CHARLES F. STANLEY BIBLE STUDY SERIES

DEVELOPING INNER STRENGTH

RECEIVE GOD'S POWER
IN EVERY SITUATION

CHARLES F. STANLEY

THOMAS NELSON
Since 1798

T0053541

DEVELOPING INNER STRENGTH
CHARLES F. STANLEY BIBLE STUDY SERIES

Published in Nashville, Tennessee, by Thomas Nelson. Thomas Nelson is a registered trademark of HarperCollins Christian Publishing, Inc.

All Scripture quotations are taken from the New King James Version.® Copyright © 1982 by Thomas Nelson. Used by permission. All rights reserved worldwide.

Thomas Nelson titles may be purchased in bulk for educational, business, fundraising, or sales promotional use. For information, e-mail SpecialMarkets@ThomasNelson.com.

ISBN 978-0-310-10564-0 (softcover)
ISBN 978-0-310-10565-7 (ebook)

First Printing August 2020 / Printed in the United States of America

HB 05.25.2021

CONTENTS

THE HOPE OF GREATER STRENGTH

A great deal has been written in recent years about inner healing, emotional wounds, and reversing low self-esteem. Bookstores and online sites are filled with self-help books. However, what so many people in our world do not realize is that the Bible has been the authoritative book on healing and strengthening the human soul (mind, emotions, and will) for thousands of years. The Bible is not a self-help book but a God-will-help book. The Bible holds out the hope and promise of God's eternal help for those who humbly turn to Him.

When we are faced with times of intense emotional stress, we will eventually reach the end of our strength. While we may be tempted to think at such times that turning to God is a sign of emotional weakness—that we should somehow just "power through"—the reality is that none of us can fully heal our spirit, soul, or body. There are certain problems and conditions that are simply beyond our capacity to self-heal. The good news is that if we are followers of Christ, the end of ourselves is the beginning for God! The help that God offers us in His Word is both eternal and timely. It is highly effective and freely available to all.

This book can be used by you alone or by several people in a small-group study. At various times, you will be asked to relate to the material in one of the following four ways.

First, what new insights have you gained? Make notes about the insights you have. You may want to record them in your Bible or in a separate journal. As you reflect on your new understanding, you are likely to see how God has moved in your life.

Second, have you ever had a similar experience? You approach the Bible from your own unique background . . . your own particular set of understandings about the world that you bring with you when you open God's Word. For this reason, it is important to consider how your experiences are shaping your understanding and allow yourself to be open to the truth that God reveals.

Third, how do you feel about the material? While you should not depend solely on your emotions as a gauge for your faith, it is important for you to be aware of them as you study a passage of Scripture and can freely express them to God. Sometimes, the Holy Spirit will use your emotions to compel you to look at your life in a different or challenging way.

Fourth, in what way do you feel challenged to respond or to act? God's Word may inspire you or challenge you to take a particular action. Take this challenge seriously and find ways to move into it. If God reveals a particular need that He wants you to address, take that as His "marching orders." God will empower you to do something with the challenge that He has just given you.

Start your Bible study sessions in prayer. Ask God to give you spiritual eyes to see and spiritual ears to hear. As you conclude your study, ask the Lord to seal what you have learned so you will not forget it. Ask Him to help you grow into the fullness of the nature and character of Christ Jesus.

I encourage you to keep the Bible at the center of your study. A genuine Bible study stays focused on God's Word and promotes a growing faith and a closer walk with the Holy Spirit in each person who participates.

RECEIVING GOD'S GIFT OF INNER STRENGTH

IN THIS LESSON

Learning: How can I get rid of my emotional baggage?

Growing: What part does God play in this, and what part do I play?

When Jesus began His ministry, He announced to the people in His hometown of Nazareth, "The Spirit of the LORD is upon Me, because He has anointed Me to preach the gospel to the poor; He has sent Me to heal the brokenhearted, to proclaim liberty to the captives and recovery of sight to the blind, to set at liberty those who are oppressed" (Luke 4:18).

Jesus came to this earth to take care of our sin problem and make it possible for us to experience forgiveness and eternal life. As He said of His mission on this earth, "The Son of Man did not come to be served, but to serve, and to give His life a ransom for many" (Mark 10:45). However, in the Bible we find that Jesus also came to make us whole from the inside out. He came to provide wholeness that brings emotional, mental, and spiritual strength.

1. What comes to mind when you think of "inner strength"?

2. What new insights do you hope to gain through this study?

THE GIFT OF THE HOLY SPIRIT

Many people believe all the Lord desires is for us to be born again—that we accept Jesus as our personal Savior and then continue to believe in Him until the day when we die and go to heaven. The Lord most certainly desires this for each of us. But He wants so much more! Our lives in Christ do not end with a salvation experience. Salvation is actually just the beginning point. Spiritual growth, maturity, and inner strength are to be the norm of our lives.

The Holy Spirit is God's gift to us. He enables us to become more and more like Jesus and experience what He purchased for us on the cross in an ever deepening way. As Paul wrote, the Holy Spirit "helps in our weaknesses" and "makes intercession for us with groanings which cannot be uttered." As we submit to His work, our relationship with God is strengthened and we begin to demonstrate certain "fruit"—traits such as "love, joy, peace, longsuffering, kindness, goodness, faithfulness, gentleness, self-control" (Galatians 5:22–23).

As we bear the identity of the Holy Spirit at work in us, and display His fruit, we begin to respond to needs as Jesus would respond—with power, love, and mercy. We begin to think what Jesus would think in response to every situation and to say what He would say. Even in the most troubling times, we discover an *inner strength* and peace that we might not even realize that we possessed. This is a peace from God, "which surpasses all understanding," and guards our "hearts and minds through Christ Jesus" (Philippians 4:7).

As Jesus was preparing to return to heaven, He spoke to His disciples about this incredible power they would receive when the Holy Spirit came upon them. "He said to them, 'It is not for you to know times or seasons which the Father has put in His own authority. But you shall receive power when the Holy Spirit has come upon you; and you shall be witnesses to Me in Jerusalem, and in all Judea and Samaria, and to the end of the earth'" (Acts 1:7–8). This same power is available to each of His followers today.

3. How would you describe the work of the Holy Spirit in your life? How have you received strength from God in the past when you most needed it?

....

....

....

....

....

....

....

4. What are some areas of your life that you would like to see further strengthened?

....

....

....

....

....

....

....

....

LIFE TO THE FULL

No matter who we are, we are all "poor" in some way. We each lack something or are weaker in one area of our emotional makeup than in others. No person is strong in all areas of life at all times. Just as we are healthier physically on some days than on others, so we go through periods when we experience a weakness in our emotions.

When those times of emotional weakness come, we generally experience emotional pain. If we deal with our emotional pain as soon as it arises, receiving God's help and healing for the injury that we have suffered, this pain is generally temporary. At other times, however, the emotional pain lingers. We may not deal with it, hoping that it will go away or heal itself. We may not know how to deal with the pain, and continue to struggle on without relief. We may not believe that we should deal with the pain, thinking perhaps that pain is inevitable and a normal part of every person's life.

If you are experiencing emotional pain today, I have three thoughts that I want to share as we begin this study. *First, time will not heal your pain, but Jesus Christ can.* He will heal you in your emotions if you turn to Him and receive the strength that He offers to you. *Second, the Bible presents God's ways for dealing with emotional pain.* For this reason, you must learn what the Bible says and apply God's truth to your life. *Third, God wants you to live in emotional freedom and strength.* He wants you to be unshackled from emotional weakness or inner pain.

The results of lingering emotional pain that goes unaddressed and unhealed can be devastating to a person and to a family. Lingering or pervasive emotional weakness will sap your energy, drain away your creativity, divert your personal motivation and enthusiasm for life, and affects your relationships. If left unhealed, it can even cause serious damage to your physical health and to your overall effectiveness as a witness for Christ in this world.

None of these conditions are God's desire for you! Rather, the Lord wants you to be filled with a vitality and enthusiasm for life, be creative in every area of talent and skill that He has given, have healthy and vibrant relationships, and be an effective witness to the gospel of Jesus Christ. He wants you to have a full life. As Jesus also said of His mission on this earth, "I have come that they may have life, and have it to the full" (John 10:10).

Let me ask you several questions. *Are you lonely? Do you feel restless and frustrated? Is anxiety eating away at your joy? Do you feel burned out, insecure, broken—as if you are a failure?* These conditions are symptoms of emotional wounds that can weaken you and make you more vulnerable to manipulation by other people and attacks in the spiritual realm. These are the symptoms Jesus came to heal and to strengthen.

Remember, Jesus said that He came to heal the brokenhearted, proclaim liberty to the captives, bring sight to the blind, and set at liberty those who are oppressed. Emotional pain and weakness will cause you to feel dejected, "bound up" inside, blind to the goodness of God, and imprisoned in darkness. Jesus came to set you free and make you whole. He came to impart to you a deep, abiding, and consistent strength . . . and develop His strength within you.

5. "Peace I leave with you, My peace I give to you; not as the world gives do I give to you. Let not your heart be troubled, neither let it be afraid" (John 14:27). How does the world give "peace"? How does this differ from the peace that Jesus brings?

6. "For God has not given us a spirit of fear, but of power and of love and of a sound mind" (2 Timothy 1:7). What encouragement does this verse offer you?

SET DOWN EMOTIONAL BAGGAGE

Jesus is the Savior, the Healer, the Deliverer, and the One who makes you whole. However, there is a twofold role that you are required to play in bringing about healing of your emotions and receiving God's strength. *First, you must be willing to set down your emotional baggage.*

"Emotional baggage" refers to old feelings, thought patterns, and past experiences that continue to traumatize you every time they are triggered or recalled. Some people have become so accustomed to carrying such heavy emotional baggage they cannot imagine life without that burden. They are so familiar with emotional pain that they can't imagine life without it. In fact, the thought of letting go of something in their past is threatening to them.

In some cases, people may feel they are opening themselves up to increased vulnerability or greater accountability—which may be true. But what is *not* true is that greater vulnerability or accountability automatically leads to renewed pain. Jesus can be present in any situation to comfort, love, and nurture you when you make yourself vulnerable to Him and open up your life to receive the fullness of His love and forgiveness. Jesus is present whenever you face up to your sin and make amends. He will help you to become accountable to Him and to others, always in a framework of love and forgiveness.

There is no benefit in continuing to carry old emotional burdens. There is no good reason for hanging on to what slows you down, keeps you from being vibrantly alive and strong, or stops you from experiencing the fullness of life that God has prepared for you. On the other hand, there is every good reason to set down your emotional baggage at the foot of the cross and to walk forward in your life with a new freedom to your step!

Today is a great day to come to the Lord and say, "Jesus, I am at the end of my ability to heal my own emotions. I cannot make myself strong. I lay down my emotional burdens, pain, and weakness at Your feet, and with Your help I resolve never to pick them up again."

7. "If anyone is in Christ, he is a new creation; old things have passed away; behold, all things have become new" (2 Corinthians 5:17)? What does it mean to be a "new creation" in Christ? What "old things" have now passed away?

8. "One thing I do, forgetting those things which are behind and reaching forward to those things which are ahead, I press toward the goal for the prize of the upward call of God in Christ Jesus" (Philippians 3:13–14). What are some things you need to "forget" and leave behind you so you can press on toward the life that God wants you to have?

LET THE LORD DO HIS PART

There is another step you must be willing to take to bring about the healing of your emotions and receive God's strength: *you must invite the Lord to do His work in your life.* The Holy Spirit will not overstep the boundaries of your will. God will not invade your life and strip away painful memories or heal your withered emotions unless you ask Him to do this work in you.

Today is a great day for asking the Lord Jesus to take from your heart the emotional load that you are carrying! He wants to heal your emotional wounds, bind up your emotional pain, and set you free from emotional bondage. *Your past and present do not need to continue into your future.* What is a reality today does not need to be what will be the reality of tomorrow.

If you are feeling unloved, you can feel love. If you are weighed down under a load of guilt, you can receive forgiveness. If you are wallowing in a cloud of confusion, you can experience God's wisdom and guidance. If your life is in turmoil, you can have peace in your heart. If you are rejected, you can be accepted and surrounded by genuine Christian friends.

God created you with a great potential for good and God desires to help you fulfill your potential. Your future can be better than your past or present. You can grow and develop and be ever more transformed into the likeness of Jesus Christ. You can experience greater fulfillment and wholeness than you are presently. You can have an even more abundant life than the one you presently have.

Those who are discouraged tend to feel they are locked into their present position—emotionally, spiritually, physically, materially. God has the keys to your prison. He can make a way out of your present circumstances and situation where you do not see a way. He can sovereignly change hearts and remove roadblocks.

The message of God's goodness is that you *can* survive the assaults of the devil against your life, endure the persecution that comes your way, be victorious over the circumstances that assail you, and—in the midst of any kind of trial, trouble, or tribulation—know God's peace and joy. You have the hope of Christ within you . . . and you also have the omnipotent power of the Holy Spirit at work within you.

So today, invite Christ to begin a healing work within you. Simply pray, "Lord Jesus, I ask You to heal me and make me strong in emotions, mind, and will. Please give me the courage to walk through life without the pain, insecurities, frustrations, and alienation that I have been feeling. I trust You to set me free, make me whole, and keep me strong."

Today is a day for new beginnings toward a stronger tomorrow!

9. "Behold, I will do a new thing, now it shall spring forth; shall you not know it? I will even make a road in the wilderness and rivers in the desert" (Isaiah 43:19). What new thing do you long for the Lord to do in your life?

10. How have you invited God to begin that healing work within you? What do you need to do if you haven't yet taken this step?

TODAY AND TOMORROW

Today: God wants me to be free of my past and move
into the future that He has in store for me.

Tomorrow: I will seek God's help in letting go of
my emotional baggage.

CLOSING PRAYER

Father, we thank You for loving us so gently, kindly, and with patience beyond our understanding. Be with us today as we begin to evaluate the emotional baggage we have been carrying with us through life—baggage that has only been weighing us down. Help us to leave our past at your feet so we can press on toward the life you intend for us. Thank You for being so willing to provide everything we need. We love You, praise You, and thank You for being the kind of loving Father who is ready and willing to help us.

NOTES AND PRAYER REQUESTS

Use this space to write any key points, questions, or prayer requests from this week's study.

STRENGTH IN TIMES OF LONELINESS

IN THIS LESSON

Learning: What can I do to not feel so lonely?

Growing: How can I gain more friends?

I have met hundreds of people over the years who have felt utterly alone, abandoned, and ostracized from society. Such feelings of loneliness are excruciating, and nearly every person alive today tries to avoid them at all costs. Even so, loneliness is pervasive in our world today.

Older people today frequently express their loneliness, especially after the death of a spouse. Divorced people say they are lonely. Young people say they are lonely, and social media convinces them that they are alone in such feelings—that everyone else "has it together." Salespeople who travel frequently are lonely. Parents who stay at home all day long with young children speak of loneliness. Those who have empty nests are lonely. Newly retired people, who are accustomed to a wide circle of colleagues, are lonely. Loneliness abounds.

It is interesting to note the Bible actually begins by addressing the issue of loneliness. As we read in the opening chapter of Genesis, "Then God said, 'Let Us make man in Our image, according to Our likeness; let them have dominion over the fish of the sea, over the birds of the air, and over the cattle, over all the earth and over every creeping thing that creeps on the earth.' So God created man in His own image; in the image of God He created him; male and female He created them" (Genesis 1:26–27).

God created Adam and placed him in the Garden of Eden. But shortly after, the Lord says, "It is not good that man should be alone; I will make him a helper comparable to him" (2:18). So God created Eve and placed her in the Garden as well. In this way, the Lord established a picture of the fellowship that He desired for human beings to share. But we also find that God displayed His own desire for companionship, for Adam walked and talked with Him frequently. God's voice in the cool of the evening was not strange to Adam (see 3:8–9). From God's point of view, loneliness is not a desirable state.

Throughout the Old Testament, we find the Lord continuing to reach out to His people. He reveals Himself to them, desires to be with them, and communicates with them. As the prophet Samuel would later state, "The LORD will not forsake His people, for His great name's sake, because it has pleased the LORD to make you His people" (1 Samuel 12:22).

1. What is significant about the fact that God decided it was "not good" for Adam to be alone?

2. What was God's original plan for humans to be in fellowship with Him?

_____

_____

_____

_____

_____

_____

_____

_____

JESUS EXPERIENCED LONELINESS

In the New Testament, we read how Jesus developed a close relationship with His disciples. He was so concerned for them to continue in their relationship with one another after His crucifixion that on His last night with them, He spent much of the time talking about their need to remain with one another and to be as one with the Father. John records His words:

> "Let not your heart be troubled; you believe in God, believe also in Me. In My Father's house are many mansions; if it were not so, I would have told you. I go to prepare a place for you. And if I go and prepare a place for you, I will come again and receive you to Myself; that where I am, there you may be also. . . .
>
> "I will pray the Father, and He will give you another Helper, that He may abide with you forever—the Spirit of truth, whom the world cannot receive, because it neither sees Him nor knows Him; but you know Him, for He dwells with you and will be in you. I will not leave you orphans; I will come to you. . . .

"As the Father loved Me, I also have loved you; abide in My love. If you keep My commandments, you will abide in My love, just as I have kept My Father's commandments and abide in His love.

"These things I have spoken to you, that My joy may remain in you, and that your joy may be full. This is My commandment, that you love one another as I have loved you. Greater love has no one than this, than to lay down one's life for his friends" (John 14:1–3, 16–18; 15:9–13).

The close communion the Lord desires is something on which we can depend, even if everyone else abandons us. Jesus knew this to be true in His own life. On the night He was arrested and tried, He said to His disciples, "Indeed the hour is coming, yes, has now come, that you will be scattered, each to his own, and will leave Me alone." Can you hear the pain in that statement? Jesus knew what it was to be lonely. But then He went on to say, "And yet I am not alone, because the Father is with Me" (John 16:32).

Jesus knew what it was to be comforted even in the face of abandonment. In the same way, regardless of what we are facing, we can be comforted in the fact that God never abandons us. Jesus is our Friend of friends. He is with us always. He never changes, never abandons us, and never withdraws from us. He is always present. We are never alone.

3. What insight do you gain from the fact that Jesus experienced loneliness?

4. "Lo, I am with you always, even to the end of the age" (Matthew 28:20). In what way is Jesus "with you always"? If He is not physically present, what does this verse mean?

....

....

....

....

....

....

....

....

....

FEELING ALONE VERSUS BEING ALONE

For some people, being alone is a blessing, because they are continually surrounded by people. For others, being alone brings about great feelings of loneliness. For still others, loneliness is so pervasive in their souls they can feel lonely even in a room full of people.

We must continually guard our minds against the idea we are an isolated example or one-of-a-kind in our feelings of loneliness. The truth is we are *never* alone. The Holy Spirit is always present and available to us, and there are many other Christians who have experienced what we are experiencing and would like to be a friend to us. At times when we are lonely, we simply need to reach out to others and invite their presence into our lives.

The prophet Elijah once felt isolated and alone. After God gave him a great victory over the false prophets of Baal, he learned the wicked queen Jezebel was intent on taking his life. Elijah fled and ended up in a deserted wilderness. As the days wore on, he cried out to God, "The children of Israel have forsaken Your covenant, torn down Your altars, and killed Your prophets with the sword. I alone am left; and they seek to take my life" (1 Kings 19:14).

Can you hear the desperation and loneliness in Elijah's words? Not only did he feel forsaken, but he also felt all of Israel had forsaken the things that were most important to him. But the Lord replied, "Go, return on your way to the Wilderness of Damascus. . . . I have reserved seven thousand in Israel, all whose knees have not bowed to Baal" (1 Kings 19:15, 18). Elijah was truly not alone as a follower of the Lord God and a keeper of God's covenant. There were 7,000 other faithful people in the land with whom he could associate!

The same is true for us. *We are not alone.* There are more people who feel the way we feel and believe the way we believe than we presently know. We just need to seek them out!

5. "I have been very zealous for the LORD God of hosts; for the children of Israel have forsaken Your covenant, torn down Your altars, and killed Your prophets with the sword. I alone am left; and they seek to take my life" (1 Kings 19:10). What was the nature of Elijah's complaint? What factors had contributed to his feelings of loneliness?

6. "Behold, the LORD passed by, and a great and strong wind tore into the mountains and broke the rocks in pieces before the LORD, but the LORD was not in the wind; and after the wind an earthquake, but the LORD was not in the earthquake; and after the earthquake a fire, but the LORD was not in the fire; and after the

fire a still small voice" (verses 11–12). How did God reassure Elijah that He was with him and in control?

_____

_____

_____

_____

_____

_____

BE A FRIEND TO OTHERS

We are never alone when we have the Spirit of God dwelling within us. Even so, we can have a *feeling* of being alone. What should we do when we have such feelings of loneliness?

Lonely people often turn to things that create more loneliness, rather than to those things that can alleviate their feelings. They turn to drugs and alcohol, both of which tend to alienate and turn away the very people with whom they might enjoy companionship. They sometimes turn to movies, social media, and binge-watch shows . . . all of which only lead them to further isolate themselves from human-to-human communication.

The foremost antidote to feelings of loneliness is to have *good relationships with Christian people*. Remember that God said, "It is not good that man should be alone,"—then He took the necessary step to resolve the situation: "I will make him a helper comparable to him" (Genesis 2:18). We often think this verse applies only to marriage, but it can also apply to godly friendships. The Lord's desire is for us to have a close, intimate relationship with Him *and* to have satisfying and enriching personal relationships with other people.

In Proverbs 18:24, we read, "A man who has friends must himself be friendly, but there is a friend who sticks closer than a brother." The real question is whether we are *willing* to be this kind of friend to others. Are we open to accepting invitations to social events with godly people—or even invite others to join us for lunch? Are we ready to get involved with our church and various ministries within our church? Will we commit to being faithful in our participation in group functions at our church?

Serving the Lord in an active way with other believers is a wonderful way for friendships to develop. Participating in retreats sponsored by a church or outside Christian organizations, especially ones that involve other people who live in our area, can be an effective way to connect with people who share common interests with us. Christian clubs, hobby groups, and Bible study groups are especially good ways to make new friends who share an interest in similar topics. Sometimes, community learning programs or neighborhood schools offer non-academic courses in subjects such as gourmet cooking, photography, or art appreciation.

Ask the Lord to reveal the people who may be your future friends. At the same time, ask Him to bring to your mind those people whom you have neglected recently. Ask Him to show you ways that you might rekindle old friendships. Remember, friendship is a good thing! It is God's will for you to have friends. When you ask the Lord to bring good Christian friends into your life, you are asking something that is according to God's will. So look for new opportunities to arise for you to be a friend, and, in the process, for you to gain a friend.

7. "Now this is the confidence that we have in Him, that if we ask anything according to His will, He hears us. And if we know that He hears us, whatever we ask, we know that we have the petitions that we have asked of Him" (1 John 5:14–15). What does this passage teach about asking God for friends?

8. What are some traits you desire in a friend? How many of those traits do *you* have?

....

....

....

....

....

....

....

TRUST GOD TO BRING THE RIGHT FRIENDS

The apostle Paul wrote, "All things work together for good to those who love God, to those who are the called according to His purpose" (Romans 8:28). This applies to your friendships! God is the engineer of social relationships, and He has a way of bringing the right people into your life at the right times for the right purposes. Sometimes friendships last a lifetime. Sometimes they are intended only for a season of life. Regardless, you need to trust God to bring you the friends you need *right now*—and also to bring you to those who need your friendship.

Do not give up on Christian friends because you feel they have disappointed you, or withdrawn from you, or are in conflict with you. Ask your friends if you have done something to damage the friendship—for example, if you have made an inadvertent mistake, or if you have required too much of the other person, or if you have failed at being a good friend. If so, apologize to your friends and seek to make amends. Value your friendships enough to do your best to maintain them and develop them over time.

Keep in mind that your feelings will often deceive you. None of us have perfect perception—especially when we are personally involved. Ask God to help you build your life on the truth of His *Word* and the consistent reliability of His presence and power. Feelings come and go, but God's love, forgiveness, and presence are eternal and rock solid.

9. What are some of the ways you met the people who have become your closest friends? What practical ideas can you gain for finding future friends?

10. "I am persuaded that neither death nor life, nor angels nor principalities nor powers, nor things present nor things to come, nor height nor depth, nor any other created thing, shall be able to separate us from the love of God which is in Christ Jesus our Lord" (Romans 8:38–39). What comfort can this passage provide when you are feeling lonely?

TODAY AND TOMORROW

Today: God does not want me to be alone
any more than I do.

Tomorrow: I will ask the Lord to lead me to new friends
this week . . . and also to those people who need friends.

CLOSING PRAYER

Jesus, thank You for Your promise to always be with us in this life. Thank You for Your promise to never leave us nor forsake us—both in this life and in the life to come. You love us tenderly, with understanding and grace, and desire companionship and intimacy with us. Thank You for loving us so much. It is our prayer that we will come to continually sense Your presence in our lives, wherever we are, and be willing to develop that friendship with You.

NOTES AND
PRAYER REQUESTS

Use this space to write any key points, questions, or prayer requests from this week's study.

STRENGTH IN TIMES OF FEAR

IN THIS LESSON

Learning: What is the root cause of my anxieties?

Growing: How can I learn to trust God more?

As a child, my insecurities and fears were no doubt linked to the fact that I had relatively few things that were consistent. Our family moved seventeen times during the first sixteen years of my life. We never seemed to have enough—especially in my early years when my mother was struggling as a young widow to provide food and shelter for the two of us. She was solely responsible for an active, curious son, and this made her overly protective of me. She frequently said, "Don't fall down . . . watch out . . . be careful." The message to me was one of doom and gloom: "Don't take any risks . . . life is scary . . . you can get hurt."

Furthermore, I was raised with the idea that God was a stern judge who was just waiting to pounce on me when I stepped out of line. From my earliest memories, I never dreamed of doing anything bad. I was too scared of the consequences! My entire outlook on life was one of deep emotional insecurity, anxiety, and fear. It took years of living with a full understanding of God's love, tenderness, and steadfast provision for me to overcome these negative emotions.

I know I am not alone in my experience. Everywhere I look today, I find people living anxious lives. In fact, if I had just one word to describe our society, it would be *anxious*. People don't feel they can trust others. The world seems to be changing rapidly on all fronts. Old moral and ethical standards in our culture have dramatically fallen away in recent years. Today, parents, stepparents, and foster parents come and go in the lives of an increasing number of children. Spouses seem more temporary than permanent in a person's life. A life in which such fluctuations and changes are the norm is *always* an anxious life.

1. When are times in your life that you experienced prolonged periods of anxiety or fear? Looking back, what were the causes of those particular emotions?

2. Do you tend to live with a pervasive feeling of anxiety? If so, what might be some of the root causes for this feeling?

....

....

....

....

....

....

THE ROOT OF ANXIETY

Anxiety is fear of the future. We might feel anxious when we come to the conclusion the future holds no promise of change. Or when we are uncertain of what is going to happen from one moment to the next. Or when we feel we are incapable of handling a new challenge, or we set standards for ourselves that are impossible to meet, or when we are torn between the two opinions of people we trust. At times, our anxiety can even be rooted in unresolved hostility.

Jesus knew all about these causes of anxiety. In His day, people were anxious about meeting the most basic of needs. He lived in a region occupied by Rome—and the Jews never knew what Rome might do next or what new taxes and laws might be issued against them. Daily life was difficult. Thousands upon thousands lived a hand-to-mouth and day-to-day existence. Sickness and disease were rampant. Tension existed between those who considered themselves to be "Law-keeping" Jews and those who were perceived to be Law-breakers.

Yet in the midst of all this anxiety, Jesus taught His disciples, "Do not worry about your life, what you will eat; nor about the body, what you will put on. Life is more than food, and the body is more than clothing. . . . Consider the lilies, how they grow: they neither toil nor spin; and yet I say to you, even Solomon in all his glory was not arrayed like one of these. If then God so clothes the grass, which today is in the field and tomorrow is thrown into the oven, how much more will He clothe you, O you of little faith? And do not seek what you should eat or what you should drink, nor have an anxious mind. For all these things the nations of the world seek after, and your Father knows that you need these things" (Luke 12:22–23, 27–30).

Jesus makes three key points in this teaching. *First, God knows what we need.* Much of our anxiety is rooted in the belief that we must maintain control over every detail in our lives, because there is nobody else whom we can trust to know our needs and to provide for us. Yet Jesus made it clear, "Your Father knows." God knows because He cares for us with an infinite love. We are of exceedingly great value to Him.

Second, God will supply what we need. God knows what we need. He also knows by what means, at what time, and in what quantity He should supply His provisions so that our needs are met fully. He is a loving Father who only desires the best for His children.

Third, only God can alleviate our feelings of anxiety. Nobody else can ever fully know or meet this need in our lives. God alone sees the beginning and the end. He alone knows what we will need at precisely the right moment for us to do the work and fulfill the plan He has for us. God provides for us as we trust Him. His part is to meet our needs. Our part is to trust Him.

3. "Consider the ravens, for they neither sow nor reap, which have neither storehouse nor barn; and God feeds them. Of how much more value are you than the birds?" (Luke 12:24). How much more valuable are you in God's eyes than birds? Consider the price He paid for your salvation. How does this affect your areas of anxiety?

4. "Seek the kingdom of God, and all these things shall be added to you" (Luke 12:31). What does it mean to "seek the kingdom of God"? Why do you think Jesus tells you to pursue God's kingdom rather than focus on meeting your own needs?

....

....

....

....

....

....

....

THE CONSEQUENCES OF ANXIETY

So, how do we overcome anxiety? The first and foremost step is to make sure we have a personal relationship with Christ. Until Jesus is part of our lives, we will always fear the unknown. We must then recognize the Holy Spirit lives within us—and ask Him to lead us, guide us, and empower us daily to live the life that God is asking us to lead.

Everyone has moments of anxiety and fear. But a *pervasive* feeling of anxiousness and fearfulness is not God's desire for any person. So choose to put your faith in what God has done for you by sending Jesus to this earth on your behalf. Decide each day to place your trust in the Holy Spirit to lead you along life's path with confidence and hope. Believe that God alone—who has all resources available for His use—can put together a "total provision package" for you.

If you refuse to do this, you are forced to either trust in yourself or in other people. The problem with this approach is that none of us can ever fully care for ourselves, nor can we rely on any other person or institution to fully provide all that we need. When we choose to follow this course, it only leads to increased irritability and frustration with life, vacillating opinions and little decision making, repeated errors of judgment, feelings of persecution, procrastination, low productivity, and a general feeling of restless-ness and uneasiness.

Jesus referred to these consequences in a parable He taught of a farmer sowing seeds. The farmer sowed on different types of ground, some of which fell among thorns. Jesus explained, "The thorns sprang up and choked [the seed]. . . . Now he who received seed among the thorns is he who hears the word, and the cares of this world and the deceitfulness of riches choke the word, and he becomes unfruitful" (Matthew 13:7, 22).

Jesus refers to our anxieties as "the cares of this world." They choke the Word of God. Those who become self-absorbed with cir-cumstances and self-pursuits are not fully capable of taking in the Word of God. They allow the mundane responsibilities of life to over-whelm them to the point they give no thought to God's promises . . . much less rely on them in their lives.

5. Which generally cause you more anxiety: "the cares of this world" or "the deceitfulness of riches"? How do these fears in your life choke out God's Word?

6. "Trust in the LORD with all your heart, and lean not on your own understanding; in all your ways acknowledge Him, and He shall direct your paths" (Proverbs 3:5–6). What does it mean to "lean on your own understanding"? Give some practical examples.

Reversing the Trend

How can we reverse this trend? Paul says we must "[bring] every thought into captivity" that is contrary to the Word of God (2 Corinthians 10:5). We must recognize our self-absorbed thoughts, capture them, and literally force them into submission. We must say, "I will not think about this. Rather, I will think about what God says in His Word. I will focus completely on the truth of God, not the facts and opinions that others are feeding me about my situation."

The words other people speak in our lives always contain an element of error, because those words are rooted in humanity and tainted by human frailty. Such words are also temporary, because no person can see the future or the past. However, what we read in God's Word is true and eternal. As Paul wrote, we must wield God's Word as a weapon, "casting down arguments and every high thing that exalts itself against the knowledge of God, bringing every thought into captivity to the obedience of Christ" (2 Corinthians 10:5).

There are several practical steps you can take to "reverse the trend" and bring your anxious thoughts into conformity with God's Word. *First, read the Gospels.* Calm your spirit by reading aloud the words of Jesus and the accounts about Him in the Gospels. Focus especially on what Jesus taught and said. Don't allow yourself to become distracted or to give up in your reading of God's Word until you feel the panic subside and a calmness take root in your heart.

Second, read the promises of God. Look up and read aloud the promises of God's Word that pertain to your situation. If you don't know those promises, refer to a topical concordance or an online source to find them. (For example, look up a word that relates to your problem, or look up those passages under the heading, "fear not.")

Third, memorize God's promises. Memorize several of God's promises that seem especially appropriate for your situation. Read the Bible daily to discover other relevant passages and also seek to memorize them. Any time that fear attempts to rise up again, recite those promises from God's Word—repeatedly, if need be—until the fear subsides.

Fourth, ask the Holy Spirit to take control. Ask the Holy Spirit to make His promises real in your life. Ask Him to take control over the situations that are causing you to fear.

Fifth, praise God. Praise the Lord for His goodness and His tender loving care over you in the past. Recall instances in which God has shown Himself to be faithful. Remember instances in which your needs were met, your heart was blessed, and you knew God was in control of your life.

Once you do this, be sure to continue to praise God for who He is and what He has done. Express your gratitude to God that He is always faithful—which means that what He has done in the past, He will do in the present and the future. Praise Him for His goodness and that He can and does work all things together for your eternal good. Praise God for His love that is infinitely deeper and more wonderful than you can fathom.

This discipline will put a stop to anxiety in your life. It will reverse the spiraling trend that can so quickly plunge you into panic or confusion. It will pull your heart and mind back into a proper focus on Jesus and what He did for you on the cross, on the Holy Spirit and what He does for you each day, and on God's power to take care of you now and forever. It will give you a basis in which to root your hope and faith. And it will invite the Holy Spirit to deal in a more potent way in you and through you . . . right in the midst of your anxiety.

Follow this process whenever anxiety threatens to take hold. You may need to devote some time each day to this discipline of reading, reciting, praying, and praising in order to defeat a pervasive feeling of anxiety or fear. Most of us did not become anxious in a moment, and most of us will not cease to feel anxious instantaneously.

7. "I rise before the dawning of the morning, and cry for help; I hope in Your word. My eyes are awake through the night watches, that I may meditate on Your word" (Psalm 119:147–148). How does the psalmist say fear and anxiety may actually be a blessing?

8. What does the psalmist recommend for dealing with your fears?

Staying the Course

It is critical to not become discouraged if your ability to trust God seems to wax and wane. You are only human, and your ability to trust in God is never absolute. Rather, you are to *grow* in your ability to trust God by choosing each day to trust God a bit more.

In times of weakness, choose to trust Him. When your trust level seems low, consciously choose to believe in Him more. Even when your trust level seems high, seek to trust God *even more*. The wonderful hope that you have is that the more you trust God, the more you will find God to be faithful. The more you trust God, the more He reveals that He can be trusted.

God said of Himself, "I am the LORD, I do not change" (Malachi 3:6). God's nature will not change. He will always be trustworthy. The more you cast your cares on Him, the more He will reveal how much He desires to care for you, give to you, and deliver you from all harm.

9. "My God shall supply all your need according to His riches in glory by Christ Jesus" (Philippians 4:19). What is the difference between God "supplying all your need" and "supplying all your desires"? What insight does this provide into your anxieties?

   _____

   _____

   _____

   _____

   _____

   _____

   _____

   _____

10. "I will instruct you and teach you in the way you should go; I will guide you with My eye" (Psalm 32:8). Why does God promise to

"instruct you" *and* "teach you"? What should your response be when you feel confused about the future?

....

....

....

....

....

....

....

TODAY AND TOMORROW

Today: The more I study God's Word, the deeper
my trust will grow.

Tomorrow: I will spend time this week memorizing
God's promises.

CLOSING PRAYER

Heavenly Father, thank You for the promise that as Your beloved children, we do not need to be anxious or fearful. As we hear Your voice and obey Your call, we can dwell securely and know that You have the power to overcome anything that we will face in this life. We pray that You will encourage our hearts as we go through difficult, trying, fearful, and anxious times. Remind us of the simple truth that You are aware of our situation and will see us through it.

NOTES AND
PRAYER REQUESTS

Use this space to write any key points, questions, or prayer requests from this week's study.

STRENGTH IN TIMES OF ABUSE

IN THIS LESSON

Learning: What should I do about the abuses I have suffered?

Growing: How will I find God's healing for the past, present, and future?

When I was nine years old, my mother married my stepfather. He was a man full of hostility, anger, and bitterness. Not once did I hear this man say he cared for me or loved me. I don't recall that he ever gave me anything. What I do recall are the times when he blew up in anger. He was so abusive that many nights as a teenager, I went to bed with a rifle loaded beside me and the door locked. Countless adults today can relate to my experiences. It seems that, over the last few years, the willingness of our society to confront abuse has greatly increased.

However, the definition of abuse tends to vary from one person to the next. The extent of *perceived* abuse can also vary from one period in life to the next. Verbal and emotional abuse are more difficult to define than physical or sexual abuse. What is important for our discussion in this session is that we recognize a fundamental difference between discipline and abuse.

Discipline is given in direct response to a person's actions. It is administered for the ultimate benefit of the person being disciplined. The goal of discipline is always altered behavior and a change in the way a person responds to life. Discipline is an act of love and is rooted in a desire for a person to be the best that he or she can be.

Abuse, in contrast, is frequently unrelated to a person's behavior. Totally innocent actions may trigger a violent response in an abuser. Abuse seeks to do a person harm and to inflict pain. It is not corrective. Most important, it is manipulative and based on power. At the core of abusive behavior is a desire to control someone else.

We can be certain about two things as it relates to abuse. First, it is never God's desire that His children be regularly injured, whether emotionally or physically. Intense verbal criticism, beatings, and instances of severe deprivation are not God's plan for any person. Second, it is never God's desire that His children be sexually abused. Molestation and incest are explicitly forbidden in the Scriptures.

Furthermore, God is never to blame in abusive situations. The blame rests solely with the abuser. If any underlying spiritual motivation is at work, it comes from the enemy, not from God. Jesus said clearly, "The thief [the devil] does not come except to steal, and to kill, and to destroy. I have come that they may have life, and that they may have it more abundantly" (John 10:10). God never motivates a person toward abusive behavior.

The Bible identifies at least six things that we can do in abusive situations. All of them allow the Lord to heal us from damage done to us emotionally. They also free us so that we are able to move forward in our lives without carrying the heavy baggage that results from abuse.

SEEK GOD'S GUIDANCE AND PRAY FOR AN ABUSER

First, seek God's guidance in an abusive situation. Ask the Lord, "What would You have me do?" Remember that no one answer will fit all situations. In some cases, God may tell you to move away from your abuser or direct you to receive counseling from a Bible-honoring counselor. In other cases, God may direct you to take different steps. You will need to ask the Lord for His plan for *you,* believing He will direct your path and give you the courage to follow His plans.

Second, pray for your abuser. The person who abuses you is a persecutor not only of you but also of Christ, who dwells within you. As you pray for the abuser, ask God to give you insights into the cause of the abusive behavior. These causes can help you as you intercede in prayer for the person. In my life, I later learned my stepfather had a deep anger against his own father, because he had been denied an opportunity to pursue the career he wanted as a young man. Knowing this did not change my stepfather, nor did it lessen my abhorrence for the abuse I experienced. It did, however, give me a greater compassion to pray for my stepfather.

Pray specifically that your abuser would come into a relationship with Jesus and the Lord would deal with his or her heart. Also pray for wisdom whether or not to confront your abuser with the message, "That's enough." Abusers often expect their victims to run away and hide, cry, shrink back, or fall silent. You may find it beneficial to stand up to your abuser and say, "I am a child of God. I will no longer take your abuse. I'm trusting God to defend me. I'm turning you over to Him, and I'm trusting that He will deal with you." However, in some situations, it may not be wise or safe to approach the person who caused you such pain. As you pray, ask the Holy Spirit for His sure and certain guidance, and trust Him to lead you.

1. "If any of you lacks wisdom, let him ask of God, who gives to all liberally and without reproach, and it will be given to him. But let him ask in faith, with no doubting, for he who doubts is like a wave of the sea driven and tossed by the wind" (James 1:5–6). What do these verses say about seeking God's wisdom in an abusive situation?

2. What promises about God's wisdom does this passage provide?

3. "I say to you, love your enemies, bless those who curse you, do good to those who hate you, and pray for those who spitefully use you and persecute you, that you may be sons of your Father in heaven; for He makes His sun rise on the evil and on the good, and sends rain on the just and on the unjust" (Matthew 5:44–45). How does Jesus say that you are to treat those who do wrong against you?

....

....

....

....

....

....

....

....

FORGIVE AN ABUSER AND BE OPEN TO GOD'S HEALING

A third step to take is to forgive your abuser. Choose to forgive the person who has abused you, and also any person who contributed or "stood by" as you were abused. As you do this, remember that forgiveness does not mean the abuse didn't happen, nor does it mean the abuse was insignificant in your life. What forgiveness does mean is that you are "letting go" of any anger, hurt, bitterness, or pain associated with the abuse. You are trusting God to deal with your abuser. Forgiveness is releasing the person—not to "go free" without any consequences, but giving that person into the hands of the Lord to reap *His* consequences. Part of forgiveness is not taking revenge into your own hands. Leave all acts of vengeance to God.

Fourth, open yourself to God's healing. Many people who have been abused continue to suffer from nightmares or memories for years after the abuse occurred. If you are experiencing continual turmoil due to the abuse, it is vitally important for you to develop a habit of filling your mind with God's Word, especially just before you go to bed at night. Listen to messages—either spoken or in song—that fill your mind with God's Word and statements of His love, goodness, and grace toward you. Listen to the Bible on audio or read aloud from God's Word.

If memories of abuse continue to haunt you, address them in the name of Jesus, saying, "Lord, I am trusting You to turn my thoughts toward what is good, right, and beneficial for me." Speak to your dreams or memories: "You are not of God, and you no longer have a place in my mind. I give you over to Christ Jesus, and I choose to think of what He has done for me rather than what has been done to me by others." Ask the Lord to replace your bad memories of abuse with positive images of the ways in which He has extended His love to you.

4. "Be kind to one another, tenderhearted, forgiving one another, even as God in Christ forgave you" (Ephesians 4:32). How often does God forgive *your* sins? How often might you have to choose to forgive others?

5. "Finally, brethren, whatever things are true, whatever things are noble, whatever things are just, whatever things are pure,

whatever things are lovely, whatever things are of good report, if there is any virtue and if there is anything praiseworthy—meditate on these things" (Philippians 4:8). In your own words, what are some things that are *true, noble, just, pure, lovely,* and *of good report?*

6. What are some things on which you can meditate when unwelcome thoughts or memories flood your mind?

PURSUE THE TRUTH
AND MOVE FORWARD

A fifth step is to pursue the truth about yourself. Those who are abused almost always come to believe lies about themselves at some point. They believe that they somehow deserved the abuse, or that they are unworthy of love, or that they are inept or incapable of succeeding in life. These are all lies . . . and they need to be labeled as such!

Rather, you must proclaim the truth about yourself: "I *can* do all things through Christ Jesus. I *am* a joint heir in Christ Jesus of all God's benefits. I *am* in line to receive God's rewards. Christ in me *does have* the power, strength, and ability. Together, we *will* succeed in this."

Every person has room for growth and improvement, but abusers rarely focus on specific areas of fault or error. Rather, abusers give generalized "labels" to their victims, using such phrases as, "You always," "You never," or, "You will never." Labels such as these are a sure indicator that a lie is being told, because the truth of God is that we all can become more than we are today. We *can* be forgiven, and God holds out hope for us that tomorrow can be brighter than today. So, every time such a negative self-criticism comes to mind, you need to respond, "That's a lie! I will not believe that. It isn't true according to God's Word."

Sixth, choose to move forward positively. Believe that God will bring something good out of your experience. Never let an abuser dictate the course of your life or keep you from doing what God is leading you to do. Part of moving forward in your life is believing the cycle of abuse in your life has been broken—and is being broken—by your change of behavior. Declare, "That may be the way I was or the situation I was in, but I am redeemed by Christ Jesus. I am in the process of being transformed into His image. I am in the process of being healed."

Always trust God to bring something good out of an abusive situation. The Lord truly can create something wonderful in you and through you, no matter how you may have been hurt by others in the past. He can make you strong where you are weak, whole in areas where you feel shattered, and healthy in areas where you have been injured.

7. "These . . . things the LORD hates . . . a false witness who speaks lies, and one who sows discord among brethren" (Proverbs 6:16,

19). How is it a lie when someone says that you are worthless or a failure? How do such lies "sow discord among brethren"?

8. "And we know that all things work together for good to those who love God, to those who are the called according to His purpose" (Romans 8:28). Why does Paul say that "all things *work together* for good" rather than "all things *are* good"?

SPEAK GOD'S LOVE TO YOURSELF

If you are a victim of abuse, let me assure you that you are loved by God, you are loved by your fellow Christians, and you are worthy to be loved. This is not because of what you have done or what has been done to you, but because of *who you are*. You are a child of God, fully adopted into His family, and fully deserving of the love of your fellow brothers and sisters in Christ.

If nobody else is around to speak the Lord's love into your life, I encourage you to speak it to yourself today. Say aloud, "I am God's child. He loves me. Yes, me!" Let the truth of those words sink deep into your soul. Let them heal the hurt you have known and the shame you have felt. Let God's love for you wipe away your tears and restore you to wholeness today.

9. "If your enemy is hungry, give him bread to eat; and if he is thirsty, give him water to drink; for so you will heap coals of fire on his head, and the LORD will reward you" (Proverbs 25:21–22). What does it mean to "heap coals of fire" on another person's head? Why does the Lord reward you when you do this?

10. "Do not be overcome by evil, but overcome evil with good" (Romans 12:21). What are the dangers in allowing what happened in the past to overcome you? What does it mean in your life to "overcome evil with good"?

TODAY AND TOMORROW

Today: Being healed of abuse involves seeing
myself as God sees me.

Tomorrow: I will deliberately choose to forgive those who have
abused me right now—and again as needed in the future.

CLOSING PRAYER

*Lord Jesus, You are our great comforter and liberator from bondage. Today,
we pray that You would comfort every single hurting, injured, and abused
person with Your grace, mercy, and love. Grant us the faith to believe that
You represent the first step toward all healing . . . and that you represent every
other step that we will take all along the path. Great Physician, heal Your
children today from the wounds of the past, and truly set us free.*

NOTES AND
PRAYER REQUESTS

Use this space to write any key points, questions, or prayer requests from this week's study.

STRENGTH IN TIMES OF CRITICISM

IN THIS LESSON

Learning: Am I really a failure if that is what I've always been told?

Growing: How can I find out what is really true about me?

Each of us experiences criticism from time to time. In some cases, it is a part of discipline to teach us how to improve in a particular skill, attitude, or behavior. Pervasive criticism, however, can have a wounding and weakening effect.

Through much of my childhood, I received messages that reinforced the idea I wasn't good for anything, wasn't worth anything, and would never amount to anything. I tried hard to please, but several factors worked against me. One was that I had started school a year before my peers, so I was always the youngest person in my class, and I also tended to be the smallest and skinniest. Another was that my mother made me wear short pants until I went to junior high school—and then I wore knickers and long socks. Nobody else wore knickers! Yet another was that I grew up in a poor environment. Several of our apartments were in the basements of buildings. From my perspective as a child, everybody was "higher" than we were.

I did have some positive influences that counterbalanced these negative messages. In particular, a schoolteacher named Mrs. Ferrell and a Sunday school teacher named Craig Stowe gave me important signs of approval when I needed them desperately. They were like beacons in a wilderness of disapproval.

Many people today carry emotional baggage associated with intense or pervasive criticism. They express it by saying, "Nobody cared," or, "I never heard a word of praise when I was growing up," or, "Nobody ever said I was doing a good job." They express the criticism they heard as children in a wide variety of self-demeaning actions or in self-deprecating statements. Such self-criticism will *damage* us on the inside. It will wound us in our emotions.

1. When in your life have you been the recipient of ongoing and intense criticism?

2. What happens to a person who is severely criticized over a prolonged period of time?

....

....

....

....

....

....

....

....

GET THE RIGHT OPINION

Criticism is nearly always registered at what we are not doing right
or what desirable qualities we seem to be lacking. Such a perceived
lack of goodness brings about a perceived state of badness. It is no wonder those who are criticized over a long period come to the conclusion, "I'm worthless. I'm no good. I can't make it. I'll never do any
better." They have been fed a message of what they *aren't* so often that
they have lost all sight of what they *are*.

Given this, the first step in overcoming the emotional wounds
of criticism is to get the right perspective on our true worth. If we continue to hold a feeling of inadequacy and low value in ourselves,
we are basically denying everything that God Himself says about us.
On the other hand, when we set our eyes on who God says we are and
what He thinks about us, we begin to gain a biblical (and truthful)
perspective on our inherent value.

God bases our worth not on *what* we have but on *whom* we have—
on Jesus Christ as our Savior and the Holy Spirit as our ever-present
Comforter and Counselor. If we have accepted Jesus as our Savior,
we have *all it takes* to have everlasting value in God's eyes! God bases
our worth not on our performance or achievements but on whether

we have received His free gift of grace and forgiveness in our lives. God bases our worth not on where we live or how we look but on whether we know, follow, and trust Jesus Christ as our Lord.

As long as we base our value on personal achievements, associations, or wealth, our perception of worth will remain low. But when we base our worth solely on our relationship with God, our perception of our value will soar! When we look at what we have done and can do by ourselves, we inevitably come to the conclusion we are lacking in ability. But when we look at all that God wants us to do, equips us to do, and promises to enable us to do, we find we lack no ability. When it comes to who we are and what we are destined to do in life, there is only one opinion that truly matters—God's opinion!

3. "Therefore, if anyone is in Christ, he is a new creation; old things have passed away; behold, all things have become new" (2 Corinthians 5:17). What does it mean that you are a "new creation" in Christ? What are the "old things" you have put behind you?

4. If you are a new creation in Christ, what does that say about any criticism you have received in the past? What does it say about criticism you may receive in the future?

DISCOVER GOD'S OPINION OF YOU

This brings us to the key question of what God's opinion is of you according to His Word. *First, God says that you are His workmanship.* As Paul writes, "We are His workmanship, created in Christ Jesus for good works, which God prepared beforehand that we should walk in them" (Ephesians 2:10). You are of notable excellence solely because God made you. You are a prized example of His creation. God looked at all that He made and declared, "It is good." That is the way the Lord looks on you as His creation. He doesn't make inferior or worthless human beings. He is a master Craftsman who produces only valuable people.

Second, God says He removed your sin nature the moment you believed in Christ as your Savior. The only thing about your creation that can keep you from the presence of God is the sin nature with which you were born. However, once you received Jesus as your Savior, that sin nature was changed. You were "born again" with a new spiritual nature that put you into a completely reconciled relationship with God. The one negative aspect of your being has been forever removed! You are valuable to the Lord as His creation. You are also forgiven and gain full status as one whom the Lord can use and bless fully for His purposes.

Third, God says He has created and saved you for a future of good works. The Lord has already designed what those good works are to be. God had a purpose in mind for you even before you were born. He has a role for you to fill and a place for you to live as His child on this earth. Furthermore, with the Holy Spirit living in you, the Lord declares that you are equipped, empowered, and enabled to succeed in all that He calls you to do.

For these reasons, refuse to perpetuate a cycle of criticism. Those who have been hurt by criticism in the past tend to be critical of others or to continue the pattern of criticism by belittling themselves. Ask the Lord to help you put a stop to both patterns. Refuse to ridicule others. Instead, choose to praise and encourage them, building up their strengths. Focus on their assets and positive attributes rather than their deficits and flaws.

The person who praises the good work of the Lord in others is an *edifier*—one who builds up others and encourages them in their faith walk. We are called repeatedly in the Scriptures to be edifiers. So choose to build up others rather than tear them down. Also refuse to disparage yourself in the presence of others or to engage in behaviors that send a message that you do not care about your appearance, reputation, or responsibilities.

5. "I have been crucified with Christ; it is no longer I who live, but Christ lives in me; and the life which I now live in the flesh I live by faith in the Son of God, who loved me and gave Himself for me" (Galatians 2:20). Why did Jesus love *you* enough to die for you? What bearing does this have on the criticisms of other people?

6. "Let all bitterness, wrath, anger, clamor, and evil speaking be put away from you, with all malice. And be kind to one another, tenderhearted, forgiving one another" (Ephesians 4:31–32). What are some practical examples of wrath, anger, clamor, evil speaking, or malice? What examples can you provide of the *opposite* behaviors?

GET THE RIGHT PERSPECTIVE ON PERFECTION

Those who experience years of criticism often strive for perfection in an effort to prove themselves worthy to others. Perfectionists are less likely to appraise their abilities and attributes realistically. They feel they are worth nothing and incapable of anything but failure, so they seek to succeed at all costs. But the truth is nobody can live up to God's perfection. No one can "get it right" all the time, live a totally sin-free life, or escape all temptation. As Paul clearly states, "*All* have sinned and fall short of the glory of God" (Romans 3:23).

This raises an important question: *What about all those verses in the Bible that call us to be perfect?* Actually, when the Bible speaks of *perfection*, it is referring to what we call *wholeness*. To be perfect, a person has to be whole—and to be made whole is to be made perfect. God calls us to pursue wholeness at all times. But the Lord also tells us in His Word that He is the One who makes us whole. We cannot make ourselves whole.

The way to "perfection," therefore, is to trust God to do His perfecting work in us. We are not to struggle to become perfect or knock ourselves out trying to get everything right all the time. He will do the appropriate work within us and bring about His perfection in His timing, using His methods, and all for His purposes.

The apostle John wrote, "My little children, these things I write to you, that you may not sin." But he was quick to continue: "And if anyone sins, we have an Advocate with the Father, Jesus Christ the righteous" (1 John 2:1). It's as if God is saying, "I don't want you to sin. I've given you My Word so that you can grow up and avoid sinning. But if and when you sin, I've made provision for that, too." So recognize you aren't who you once were and that the Lord is continuing to mold and make you. Trust Him to be your potter (see Jeremiah 18:1–6).

7. "And He said to me, 'My grace is sufficient for you, for My strength is made perfect in weakness.' Therefore most gladly I will rather boast in my infirmities, that the power of Christ may rest upon me" (2 Corinthians 12:9). When have you seen the strength of God "made perfect" in your own life through your weakness?

8. How can you use this verse as an answer to those who criticize you unfairly? How can you use it to stop striving for perfection?

Have the Right Desire to Please

Those who have suffered from criticism often have a great desire to please others. They go above and beyond the call of duty in an attempt to gain the approval of those in authority over them. As believers in Christ, we are always called to do our best with the talents and gifts that God has given us. However, we are *not* called to compare ourselves to others in the hopes that, "by comparison," we will look better. Nor are we called to seek the approval of others if that approval is contrary to God's commandments.

God doesn't grade on the curve. He always judges our behavior against the absolute standard of His commandments. Furthermore, He is not merciful on the basis of whether other people like us but solely on the basis of our acceptance of Jesus Christ. We gain nothing by comparing ourselves to others or seeking to win popularity among our peers. Rather, we should desire to allow the Holy Spirit to transform us, be willing to trust God where He chooses to lead, and commit to do what the Lord calls us to do, even if it is contrary to the values of the world.

To truly please God, we must be willing to change and to grow ever more into the likeness of Christ. The Lord doesn't ask us to succeed in the eyes of others, but He does ask us to live a life that is acceptable to Him. Jesus never said, "Do your best." He said, "Follow Me." If we truly desire to please the Lord, we will follow Him and become His disciples.

9. "Do not be conformed to this world, but be transformed by the renewing of your mind, that you may prove what is that good and acceptable and perfect will of God" (Romans 12:2). What does it mean to be conformed to this world? How does the renewal of your mind help you to discover God's perfect will for your life?

10. "For you were once darkness, but now you are light in the Lord. Walk as children of light (for the fruit of the Spirit is in all goodness, righteousness, and truth), finding out what is acceptable to the Lord" (Ephesians 5:8–10). If you are walking in the light of Christ, what value can other people's criticism have?

TODAY AND TOMORROW

Today: God's perspective of me is the only one that matters, and I must think of myself as He thinks of me.

Tomorrow: I will study God's Word this week, deliberately striving to renew my mind.

CLOSING PRAYER

Father, thank You for making us the way we are right now . . . just as we are. You do not make any mistakes, nor do You make anything inferior. We know today that we are Your children—Your sons and daughters—and You have made each of us in Your image. Help us never to forget that truth. Today, we want to trust You, and follow You, and rest in the wonderful love You have directed toward us. We choose to leave all our feelings behind and accept who we are in Christ. Thank You for releasing all of us from any feelings that do not belong in our lives.

NOTES AND
PRAYER REQUESTS

Use this space to write any key points, questions, or prayer requests from this week's study.

STRENGTH IN TIMES OF GUILT

IN THIS LESSON

Learning: What is the meaning of my constant guilt feelings?

Growing: How can I find lasting freedom from sin and guilt?

Most people develop their concept of God based on their perceptions of their parents. My father died when I was nine months old. When he died, a concept of God was established in my life that said, in effect, "God has left you as well." My mother worked full-time, and I spent many hours alone after school. I came to believe God was away somewhere with somebody else. He was remote to me, and from my perspective as a lonely and anxious child, He was harsh. In truth, I viewed him much like my stepfather: mean, abusive, and out to put me down.

I had seen God's hand at work in my church and in my grandfather's life to the point that I had the faith to believe in Him. I knew the Bible stories well enough to know about Jesus and what He had done in giving His life on the cross. Still, God was such a mystery that I never felt He was accessible to me. I had a strong feeling that I needed to be more *holy* so that God might come closer. No matter how much I read the Bible, I felt I could have read it more. No matter how much I prayed, I felt I could have prayed more. I felt certain God was keeping score on my behavior. The end result was the heavy emotional baggage of pervasive guilt.

Over the years, many people have told me they had a similar experience in their lives. They spent years trying to be good enough for God to approve of them. They tried to perform for God so that He might reward them. They strove to do enough good works to earn His favor. However, the good news of the gospel is that we are not saved according to our works but according to the grace of God. We can never earn our salvation. It is a free gift from God.

As Paul states, "If you confess with your mouth the Lord Jesus and believe in your heart that God has raised Him from the dead, you will be saved. For with the heart one believes unto righteousness, and with the mouth confession is made unto salvation" (Romans 10:9–10). The provision for our salvation has been made in full by Jesus Christ. There's nothing more that we can add to it. We can only receive this free gift of God's mercy and love.

1. What is your perception of God? Do you see him as distant and stern or close and loving? How do you think you formed these beliefs about God?

2. What are some ways that you have struggled with feelings of guilt in the past?

_____

_____

_____

_____

_____

_____

THE REALITY OF OUR SINFUL NATURE

I would like to tell you that after I received Jesus at the age of twelve, all feelings of guilt were completely removed from my life. But that was not the case. The emotional baggage of pervasive guilt continued to manifest itself periodically in my life.

This does not mean my salvation was invalid. I have absolutely no doubt my conversion was genuine, my spiritual nature was changed, and my heart was cleansed on that day. However, what I had to face was what all Christians have to face—that we continue to sin, break God's commandments, and give in to temptation even after we are born again. In my years as a pastor, I have concluded that most Christians don't know what to do when they continue to sin after salvation. So let's take a look at what the Bible has to say.

First, the Bible says that after we have experienced God's free gift of grace, our desire for sin diminishes. Paul wrote, "What shall we say then? Shall we continue in sin that grace may abound? Certainly not! How shall we who died to sin live any longer in it?" (Romans 6:1–2). Our desire for sin is greatly diminished when we experience God's forgiveness.

Second, the Bible acknowledges that we sin even after we are born again. Paul also admitted to the Romans, "What I am doing, I do not understand. For what I will to do, that I do not practice; but what I hate, that I do" (Romans 7:15). It is in those times we must say to God,

"I'm struggling. Please forgive me and help me." Forgiveness is granted to the Christian the moment it is requested. Our feelings of being forgiven, however, may take some time.

Third, the Bible says we grow in our understanding of God's grace. Peter encouraged, "Grow in the grace and knowledge of our Lord and Savior Jesus Christ" (2 Peter 3:18). The more we become like Christ and are conformed to His will and likeness, the more we realize the awesome nature of God and how great the gulf was between us and Him. Our salvation becomes an ever-increasing miracle to us. We have an increasing desire to guard our hearts against the temptations of the devil because our salvation is so precious to us.

Fourth, the Bible teaches that every time we have an awareness of our sin, we are to ask for God's forgiveness. There never is a time when we should feel we are beyond God's ability to forgive us. I have met Christians who say, "I've sinned so many times since I was saved that I'm not sure if God will forgive me one more time." The reality is that God forgives all our sin all the time. We cannot fathom such mercy, but nonetheless it is real. Surely, if Jesus taught His disciples they were to forgive others up to "seventy times seven" for sins committed against them (Matthew 18:22), our heavenly Father is able to forgive us that many times and more!

3. "If we confess our sins, He is faithful and just to forgive us our sins and to cleanse us from all unrighteousness" (1 John 1:9). What sins does John say are covered? Are there sins you could commit to which this verse does *not* apply?

4. "Peter came to Him and said, 'Lord, how often shall my brother sin against me, and I forgive him? Up to seven times?' Jesus said to him, 'I do not say to you, up to seven times, but up to seventy times seven'" (Matthew 18:21–22). What does this passage say about God's ability and willingness to forgive all your sins?

LET GO OF THE PAST

Once we have requested God's forgiveness, the next step in being free from guilt is to let go of our past. During my ministry, I have met countless people who are haunted by their sins. They have not been able to forgive themselves and let go of their past failures. Yet the Bible tells us that once we have repented of our sins, God forgives them and forgets them (see Isaiah 43:25).

It is not the Lord who reminds us of past sins we have already confessed to Him. Rather, it is the evil one the Bible calls the "accuser of our brethren," who is the devil (Revelation 12:10). When we are confronted with memories of sins we have already confessed, it's time to say, "I refuse to accept these thoughts. God has already forgiven me. I'm letting this go."

Furthermore, we must remember that sins and mistakes are different from each other. A sin is a choice to do something we know is against God's will. It is a willful act—one that is calculated, thought out, anticipated, and fully conceived on our part. It is deliberately flying in the face of what we know is right in God's eyes.

A mistake is usually spur-of-the-moment, unplanned, and made without forethought. A mistake is a miscalculation or an error in judgment. We are to own up to our mistakes and learn from them. We are to make amends if we have hurt anyone in making our mistakes. We are to ask God to help us not to make the same mistake again. We are not to beat ourselves up over the mistakes we make. To err is human. As long as we are alive, we are going to make mistakes.

We are also to avoid feelings of false guilt, which occurs when we take on the guilt that appropriately belongs to another person. This kind of guilt is often experienced by those who are the victims of abuse or rejection. Parents whose adult children rebel against God's Word also tend to feel this guilt. They feel they must have failed in some way and have contributed to the rise of their children's sinful behavior.

If you are holding on to such false guilt, you must let go of it. Ask the Lord to free you from all guilt that is associated with sins that are not your own.

5. "I, even I, am He who blots out your transgressions for My own sake; and I will not remember your sins" (Isaiah 43:25). What kind of record does this verse say God keeps of your past sins? What kind of record do *you* keep?

6. When have you struggled with guilt over mistakes? When have you struggled with false guilt? How has the Lord dealt with you in each case?

_____

_____

_____

_____

_____

_____

_____

_____

DON'T WORRY YOU'VE MISSED GOD'S CALL

Some people feel they have missed something God wanted them to do—that the Lord called them to do something for Him and they failed to do it. They feel guilty as a result. I always encourage these people to ask themselves two questions. The first question is: *Was the call really from God, or was it something from your own desire?* If the call was not from God, the Lord does not hold them responsible for fulfilling it.

The second question is: *Did you have an opportunity to fulfill that call and turn away from it?* In some cases, people feel a rather vague call of God toward a particular area of service, but an opportunity never presented itself to become involved in that area of ministry. These individuals should feel no guilt for having "failed" God.

Sometimes, these people respond that they did feel a specific call from God and had a specific opportunity to fulfill it, but they chose a different course of action. In such cases, I advise that today is the day to turn to the Lord and say, "I'm sorry that I disobeyed You. I ask You to forgive me. Whatever You want me to do from this point on, I'll do it."

We can all take heart from the life of Jonah. He had a specific call and turned his back on it, but God gave him a second chance. He will do the same in our lives.

7. "There are many plans in a man's heart, nevertheless the Lord's counsel—that will stand" (Proverbs 19:21). What does this verse say about the plans that humans make? How can you know that God's plans for your life will never fail?

8. "Draw near to God and He will draw near to you" (James 4:8). What steps do you need to take today if you have failed to follow God's plans?

HAVE AN ACCURATE CONCEPT OF GOD

Many people suffer from a pervasive feeling of guilt. I have also experienced this feeling in the past. Yet such feelings have nothing to do with what we know to be true from the Bible or what it means to be saved or forgiven. It is a feeling rooted in our perception of God.

As I shared earlier, I grew up believing God to be a harsh and hard judge. I felt I had to be perfect in order for God to accept me and love me. I knew I wasn't perfect, so I had feelings of guilt that I had failed God . . . and that I continued to fail Him daily. What was wrong was not my sinful state—that had been changed the moment I accepted Jesus—but my concept of God. It took years for me to acquire an accurate concept of God and to come to the point where I could feel genuine love flowing between Him and me. I'm not talking about just saying, "I love You" to God. I'm talking about deep, intimate feelings of love both for and from God.

If you are struggling with a false perception of God, I encourage you to take a long and hard look at the Gospels. Jesus is a perfect reflection of God the Father. He didn't do anything that was contrary to the nature and desire of His heavenly Father. Jesus was tender with children. He extended forgiveness to those whom the rest of society was ready to put to death. He healed the sick. He loved others so much that He was prepared to die for their sins.

Your abusive parent is not the image of God. Nor is the teacher, coach, or other authority figure who treated you harshly. Only Jesus reflects the true image of God! It is Jesus who longs to wrap His arms around you and say, "Come with Me to visit My Father. He can hardly wait to meet you!"

God understands your frailties and weaknesses, and He loves you with a deep, unchanging love in spite of them. God's love for you is unconditional. He does not place any "ifs," "whens," or any other qualifiers on His love. So don't limit God's capacity to love. It is infinite, and it extends to you in all situations and conditions.

Refuse to trust your *feelings* about God. Instead, trust the truth presented in God's Word. Base how you feel on the sure foundation of God's love as revealed by Jesus. Only you can know if you have a right understanding of God and a right relationship with God. If you are not "right" with God, you can be. The Lord stands ready at all times to forgive you and receive you fully into His presence.

The Lord's desire is for you to be free of guilt and sin. All you need to do is to take Him up on His offer to carry the load of your guilt and sin.

9. "For God so loved the world that He gave His only begotten Son, that whoever believes in Him should not perish but have everlasting life. For God did not send His Son into the world to condemn the world, but that the world through Him might be saved" (John 3:16–17). How do you think God felt when Jesus died on the cross? What does that level of love for you suggest about God's grace?

10. "As a father pities his children, so the LORD pities those who fear Him. For He knows our frame; He remembers that we are dust" (Psalm 103:13–14). How do these verses reveal that God understands our weaknesses? How does He feel toward us regardless?

TODAY AND TOMORROW

Today: God is not taken by surprise when I sin, but
He is always ready to forgive me.

Tomorrow: I will ask the Lord to show me the difference
between legitimate guilt and false guilt.

CLOSING PRAYER

Lord, we are comforted that some of the greatest witnesses for You in Scripture were those who actually blew it the worst. We learn from their example that when we make mistakes, we must confess them to You, repent, and change. Thank You for Your love toward us when we take that step. Help us to lay down the guilt we have been carrying and place it at Your feet. Take the jailhouse door off our backs so we can stand up straight and know we have been made righteous by Your grace through the blood of Jesus. We ask this in Your precious name.

NOTES AND PRAYER REQUESTS

Use this space to write any key points, questions, or prayer requests from this week's study.

STRENGTH IN TIMES OF FRUSTRATION

IN THIS LESSON

Learning: What is the cause of life's countless frustrations?

Growing: How do I overcome an ongoing frustration with life?

There was never a time when I felt God say directly to me, "I want you to preach." But from the time I was saved, I never really thought about doing anything else. To me, preaching always seemed to be what I was destined to do.

I came to adulthood with a heavy load of emotional baggage—lots of insecurities and a lifelong feeling of loneliness—so being a pastor was probably one of the least likely things I *should* have aspired to do. Being a pastor meant dealing with many different people, and I had virtually no experience in how to accomplish that feat. It also meant being in a leadership position, and again, nothing in my background had prepared me for such a role.

In my feelings of inadequacy, I drove myself to be the most perfect pastor who had ever lived. I studied long and hard, prayed long and hard, and worked long and hard. I drove myself—and I drove other people. I wanted God's approval, but I also wanted the approval of those who called me to be their pastor.

In other words, I did what almost all perfectionists do. *I exerted control,* because I felt that I had to be in control regardless of what was happening. *I was combative.* No matter what was going on, I was ready to fight if somebody wanted to fight—not physically, of course, but intellectually and spiritually. And *I was critical of others.* If a certain person did not live up to my high standards, I was sure to let my disapproval be known. I was wrong on all three counts. Furthermore, as a result of my actions, I became continually irritated and frustrated.

Such irritation and frustration are "inner events." As a general rule, those who possess such pervasive feelings either (1) have not dealt with something, (2) are running from something, or (3) have not identified something that they need to address in their lives. Such individuals also tend to refuse to confront their feelings of inner anger.

Irritation and frustration are often rooted in our inability to accept the way God has created us, a reluctance to face a problem in the past, or a refusal to confront something that we know is wrong and contrary to God's purposes and plan. I have met countless people who have a deep inner frustration that never seems to leave them. I usually ask them, "Why are you striving so hard? What are you expecting to earn? Is it a matter of *pride*—a desire to be recognized? Is it a matter of *control*—a search for greater power? Or is it a matter of *inadequacy*—a belief you must do more and more in order to be loved?"

If so, I have good news for you. God couldn't possibly love you more than He loves you right now. If you are attempting to earn His approval, you already have it! God's word to you is, "Let Me do the striving on your behalf. Let Me do the work in you. Receive My love and forgiveness. Receive My help. Accept My offer and let Me do My perfecting work in you."

1. When have you experienced prolonged periods of frustration in your life? What circumstances caused them? What underlying issues might have been the root cause?

2. "For by grace you have been saved through faith, and that not of yourselves; it is the gift of God, not of works, lest anyone should boast" (Ephesians 2:8–9). What does this passage say about your ability to "earn" God's approval?

GOD-GIVEN FRUSTRATION

There are times when irritability is not rooted in failure or a desire for perfection. Rather, God places a type of restlessness in your spirit. This type of frustration can be differentiated by four qualities. First, you are not trying to conquer anybody or anything. Second, the onset of the frustration is usually quite sudden and intense, even though there seems to be no cause for it. Third, the frustration is not with anybody but yourself. Fourth, the frustration ends the moment you move into the new path that God is instructing you to follow.

When this type of frustration manifests itself in your life, you should be glad! God is plowing up your soul and forcing you to confront a deeper part of your character. He is doing a good work in you that is for your growth and eternal good.

Most of us are familiar with Paul's words in Romans 8:28: "We know that all things work together for good to those who love God, to those who are the called according to His purpose." But the next two verses reveal that God's purpose in working all things for our good is so we can be transformed into the likeness of Christ: "For whom He foreknew, He also predestined to be conformed to the image of His Son, that He might be the firstborn among many brethren. Moreover whom He predestined, these He also called; whom He called, these He also justified; and whom He justified, these He also glorified" (Romans 8:29–30).

When you have a churning feeling inside you—a restlessness in your soul—consider the possibility that God is "justifying" you to conform with the image of Christ. Face up to any sins the Lord reveals to you during this time. Read God's Word with renewed vigor and be alert to verses that God may cause to leap off the page. Start expecting God to show you what He is leading you to do. Thank the Lord for getting you ready for His next step in your life!

3. When are times in your life that you experienced God-given frustrations?

....
....
....

4. "He who has begun a good work in you will complete it until the day of Jesus Christ" (Philippians 1:6). How have you seen God complete the work that He started during times of restlessness in your life?

....
....
....
....
....
....
....

FRUSTRATION ROOTED IN PERFECTIONISM

At times, frustration can lead people to engage in various compulsions and obsessions. Typically, the cause of this behavior stems from issues related to perfectionism. People feel they must attain a certain goal or reach a certain end and becoming singularly focused on that quest. In the end, such compulsions and obsessions prove to be traps rather than blessings. They drive people to pursue something until they gain it, regardless of who is hurt in the process or what damage to their relationships they might cause.

Frustration can also lead to greed, which is a form of obsession. The more people want, the more there is to want. The apostle Paul warned about this type of obsession when he wrote, "Those who desire to be rich fall into temptation and a snare, and into many foolish and harmful lusts which drown men in destruction and perdition. For the love of money is a root of all kinds of evil, for which some have strayed from the faith in their greediness, and pierced themselves through with many sorrows" (1 Timothy 6:9–10).

I have good news and bad news when it comes to your needs. The bad news is that you will never find wholeness and satisfaction in this life through material wealth. Study after study reveals the richest people in the world are also the most unhappy. More money only leads to more wants, more isolation, and more obsessive behaviors. But the good news is that God has a much better way for you. He knows exactly what you need and desires only the best for you. He knows what to give you at just the right time so that your heart remains fixed on Him.

As Paul concluded, "Now godliness with contentment is great gain. For we brought nothing into this world, and it is certain we can carry nothing out. And having food and clothing, with these we shall be content" (1 Timothy 6:6–8). Seek God first and give your desires to Him. He will help you to experience life to the fullest as you put your trust in Him.

5. "Set your mind on things above, not on things on the earth. For you died, and your life is hidden with Christ in God" (Colossians 3:2–3). What does it mean to "set your mind on things above"? How would that change your goals in life?

6. "One from the crowd said to Him, 'Teacher, tell my brother to divide the inheritance with me.' But He said to him, 'Man, who made Me a judge or an arbitrator over you? . . . Take heed and beware of covetousness, for one's life does not consist in the abundance of the things he possesses'" (Luke 12:13-15). Why did Jesus refuse to intervene on the man's behalf? What is the inherent danger of covetousness?

....

....

....

....

....

....

....

FRUSTRATION WITH OTHER PEOPLE

There are times when it is natural for us to feel frustration on a short-term basis. This frustration is often related to the actions of another person and can arise from conflicting preferences, opinions, or personality traits. Other times, it is related to circumstances that are beyond our control. What are we to do in such situations?

The Bible teaches we can experience a continual feeling of inner contentment *regardless of our outward circumstances.* When the apostle Paul penned the letter to the Philippians, he was sitting in a Roman prison and facing all kinds of persecution and ridicule from others. Yet he could still write, "I have learned in whatever state I am, to be content: I know how to be abased, and I know how to abound. Everywhere and in all things I have learned both to be full and to be hungry, both to abound and to suffer need" (Philippians 4:11-12).

How did Paul find inner contentment? By focusing on the sovereignty of God rather than on the will of people, by praising God rather than criticizing others, and by putting his trust in God to deal with the future rather than continually looking at the past. Paul put his faith in God to make things right rather than distrusting in his own human ability. He turned his attention *toward* Christ and *away* from his circumstances and detractors.

Paul's contentment did not rest in a denial of the outside world or his own situation. Rather, it flowed from his absolute trust in Christ Jesus. In the same way, the answer on how to deal with your frustrations—whether related to unresolved issues, or situations over which you have no control, or to a God-given stirring within—will come as you learn to trust in God.

7. "Be anxious for nothing, but in everything by prayer and supplication, with thanksgiving, let your requests be made known to God; and the peace of God, which surpasses all understanding, will guard your hearts and minds through Christ Jesus" (Philippians 4:6–7). What does Paul advise you to do when you are feeling anxious?

....

....

....

....

....

....

8. What promise are you given in this passage when you choose to trust in God? In what ways is this easy or difficult for you to do?

....

....

....

....

....

....

....

FRUSTRATION ROOTED IN IMPATIENCE

Finally, there are times when our feelings of frustration are rooted in a hurry-up attitude. We become impatient with the timing of certain events or changes that we desire in our lives.

Such a restlessness in our spirit can lead to a tendency to run past God's will. We may know what God wants us to do, and in our eagerness to get the job done, we forget that God also has a perfect timetable for accomplishing His will. Just as the Lord has a right *thing* for us to do, so He also has a right *time* for each step that He wants us to take.

The Bible repeatedly shows us the advantages of "waiting on the Lord." *Waiting* means saying to God, "Is now the time? I'm not going to move forward until You give me the green light." It means evaluating whether we are in a pattern of getting ahead of God's timing. We then ask ourselves, "Why do I keep running right past God's will? Why am I in such a hurry?"

The disadvantages of getting ahead of God are evident throughout the Bible. Abraham and Sarah got ahead of God's plan when they decided to produce an heir through Hagar (see Genesis 16). Peter was notorious for trying to get ahead of God's plan, even slicing off a man's ear in the Garden of Gethsemane (see John 18:10). Jesus, on the other hand, never showed up too early or too late. He always arrived right on time, in keeping with what the Father was doing. Learning to wait on God's timing is one of the hallmarks of the mature Christian life.

The Lord doesn't catapult us into greatness but grows us into spiritual maturity. He stretches us slowly so we don't break. He expands our vision slowly so we can take in all the details of what He desires to accomplish. He causes us to grow slowly so we stay balanced.

The unfolding of God's plan is a lifelong process. So relax in His presence and allow Him to lead the journey and do His work in you. He will do whatever it takes to prod you toward His higher places.

He will make you restless if it is time for you to move on. He will cause you to hunger and thirst for more of Him. He will plant within you a desire for things that you never dreamed of in your relationship with Him.

Trust God with *all* the circumstances, relationships, and schedules in your life. Rest in Him. He desires to be your strong and sure haven in all times of frustration.

9. When have you rushed ahead of God's timing? What was the long-term result?

10. "Wait on the LORD; be of good courage, and He shall strengthen your heart; wait, I say, on the LORD!" (Psalm 27:14). Why does the psalmist tell you to be of good courage when waiting on the Lord? Why is courage needed? Where do you find that courage?

TODAY AND TOMORROW

Today: Life's frustrations are God's way of building Christlike character in my life.

Tomorrow: I will spend time in Scriptures and prayer, actively seeking to keep my heart from becoming troubled.

CLOSING PRAYER

Heavenly Father, You uphold us when we cannot uphold ourselves. You sustain us when there is nothing left within us. You fill us when we are drained and there is no energy left. Your supernatural and sovereign power is there every single time. Grant us the wisdom to place our faith in the person of Jesus Christ who is, indeed, the source of our strength when we are frustrated. Remind us today that nothing will work unless You first are at work in our lives. Let us be open and willing to receive Your direction and obedient to Your call on our lives.

Notes and Prayer Requests

Use this space to write any key points, questions, or prayer requests from this week's study.

STRENGTH IN TIMES OF BURNOUT

IN THIS LESSON

Learning: What is the difference between serving others and burning myself out?

Growing: Where do I draw the line between serving God and doing too much?

During my years of striving for perfection in ministry, I knew I was working too hard for an impossible ideal and expecting too much of myself and others. However, I justified my behavior, as many perfectionists do, by saying, "God just made me this way." The result was that I got on a downward spiral of more and more work in an effort to get better and better and to receive more and more approval. Eventually, I crashed.

In 1977, I was doing two 30-minute television programs plus the Sunday morning television program that came from the church, in addition to many other things. I began to notice that instead of just being tired on Monday, I was tired on Tuesday . . . and then on Wednesday . . . and then all week. I went to the hospital three times that year and had all kinds of tests. Each time, the doctors could find nothing physically wrong with me. I would promise to take a little break, but it was never a long enough break to really help me.

The time finally came when I was so exhausted that I took the "orders" of my church board and went on a leave of absence for several months. I felt so drained that I wondered if I would ever again regain sufficient strength to function normally. In the months that followed, I did some serious introspection and came to the conclusion that the number-one person who was driving me was *me*. Prior to that time, I would have said I was doing it all because I loved God. But I realized much of what I was doing for God . . . I was really doing for *myself*.

Much of my prayer life had become focused on what I wanted to achieve and wanted to accomplish for the church. I wanted to do it all and have it all. In the end, it only left me utterly exhausted—physically, mentally, and emotionally. I know many people who have also found themselves in this situation. What about you? Have you ever felt burned out and stressed out . . . and then realized the cause of that burnout was your own unsatisfied ambition?

1. When have you experienced burnout—a feeling of total physical, mental, and emotional exhaustion? What did you do?

2. Looking back, how did the Lord work in your life at that time?

PURSUE REST AND PRACTICE CHRISTIAN DISCIPLINES

I took off twelve weeks from the church during this period of burnout. A little to my surprise, I returned to find the attendance in the church was up, the offering was up, and the people were happy. God had taken good care of His flock! It took nearly ten more months for me to feel I was fully back physically. During the course of those months, I learned four key principles that I believe are also reflected in God's Word.

First, learn to rest and pace yourself mentally, physically, and emotionally. Mental, physical, and emotional burnout are all related. So the first step toward being healed of burnout always includes a period of prolonged rest coupled with good nutrition. When you are physically exhausted, your mind and emotions are also affected.

We frequently read in the Gospels that Jesus withdrew from His disciples, from the crowds, and from His ministry to rest and to pray. Matthew relates, "When [Jesus] had sent the multitudes away,

He went up on the mountain by Himself to pray" (Matthew 14:23). Mark tells us, "Jesus withdrew with His disciples to the sea" (Mark 3:7). Luke writes, "He Himself often withdrew into the wilderness and prayed" (Luke 5:16). Jesus had a pattern of rest in His life. As His followers, we should seek to do the same.

Second, never get too busy for basic Christian disciplines. A loss of Christian disciplines—including reading God's Word, spending time in prayer, and maintaining fellowship with other believers—is one of the clearest signs that you could be facing burnout. It often indicates that you have taken on too much responsibility, are involved in too many activities, or are consumed with too many matters.

Spending time each day in *God's Word* will help you understand how to think, act, and respond to life. It will develop your nature, character, attitude, and mindset. Spending time in *prayer* is vital if you are to have a walking-and-talking intimacy with the Lord. You need to take time each day to tell God how you feel, thank Him for the good things in your life, praise Him for what He has done, and praise Him for who He is. You can share your worries, hopes, and desires and listen for Him to speak His words of comfort, counsel, and direction.

Maintaining fellowship with other believers is also vital if you want to continue to grow in your faith. Get involved in a church with those who believe God's Word the way you do. Attend regularly. Volunteer your services in an area where you can share your talents and gifts. The person who is too busy to attend church, too tired to pray, and too preoccupied to read God's Word has priorities that are out of line. Such a person is on his or her way to burnout.

3. "Six days you shall labor and do all your work, but the seventh day is the Sabbath of the LORD your God. In it you shall do no work. . . . For in six days the LORD made the heavens and the earth, the sea, and all that is in them, and rested the seventh day" (Exodus 20:9-11). Why does God command you to take a day of rest

each week? What does this suggest about your *real* motivations when you are pushing yourself too hard?

4. What does it mean that God *hallowed* the Sabbath and made it holy (see Genesis 2:3)? How can a day be holy? How should you treat a day that is holy?

5. "O God, You are my God; early will I seek You; my soul thirsts for You; my flesh longs for You in a dry and thirsty land where there is no water" (Psalm 63:1). When was the last time you could honestly say your soul thirsted for God? What can you do today to rekindle your desire for God's presence and company in your life?

SET CLEAR PRIORITIES AND TRUST OTHERS

A third key principle I learned is to make a decision to do only what the Lord requires. Many of us reach the burnout stage because we are simply trying to do too many things at the same time. We must keep in mind that God does not commit Himself to helping us do everything that we want to do in our lives. He is committed to helping us do only things He wants and calls us to do.

God spends His wisdom, knowledge, and understanding on what He wants to see accomplished in us. For this reason, He will often allow us to reach the burnout stage so we can learn (1) we are doing more than He is requiring us to do, (2) we have our priorities out of order, (3) we aren't putting Him first, and (4) we are trying to do too many things all at once.

If you are feeling worn out today, I suggest that you back off from everything and reappraise your life. Make a list of everything that you are doing and identify the time and energy required for each activity. Look for trends and patterns among the activities. Do you find a balance between mental and physical activities? Is there a balance between rest and work?

Finally, ask the Lord to reveal to you what it is that is truly important to Him. Ask Him to show you where you need to spend more time, where you need to spend less time, and which activities you might drop. Consider each activity on your list and ask Him, "Is this something that You want me to be doing right now, to this degree, and in this way?"

A fourth key principle is to trust God to help you trust others. One of the most positive lessons I learned during my time of recuperating from burnout was to yield control over certain activities and responsibilities to others on the church staff. I learned to trust God to give other people both the wisdom and the skill to fill the gaps and the energy to take up the slack in those areas of authority that I delegated. Jesus Himself serves as our role model in delegating responsibilities, as the following account in the Gospel of Mark relates:

> And He called the twelve to Himself, and began to send them out two by two, and gave them power over unclean spirits. He commanded them to take nothing for the journey except a staff—no bag, no bread, no copper in their money belts—but to wear sandals, and not to put on two tunics.
>
> Also He said to them, "In whatever place you enter a house, stay there till you depart from that place. And whoever will not receive you nor hear you, when you depart from there, shake off the dust under your feet as a testimony against them. Assuredly, I say to you, it will be more tolerable for Sodom and Gomorrah in the day of judgment than for that city!"
>
> So they went out and preached that people should repent. And they cast out many demons, and anointed with oil many who were sick, and healed them (Mark 6:7–13).

To trust others with supervisory or administrative authority in this manner, you must first be willing to share the credit for jobs done well. You must also be willing to let others have relationships that you don't share and be willing to let others make mistakes occasionally rather than to dictate that no mistakes be made. Above all, you have to be willing to see others grow in their faith and in their ability to trust in God.

6. Why did Jesus command His disciples "to take nothing for the journey except a staff" (a walking stick)? What does this suggest about your need to prepare for future problems?

7. "With what shall I come before the Lord, and bow myself before the High God? . . . He has shown you, O man, what is good; and what does the Lord require of you but to do justly, to love mercy, and to walk humbly with your God?" (Micah 6:6, 8). How would you define *acting justly, loving mercy,* and *walking humbly* with God?

8. How does this list of things "God requires" compare with your list of activities?

....

....

....

....

....

....

....

CONFRONT YOUR NEED TO DO ALL AND BE ALL

Those who avoid burnout have learned to institute several key practices into their lives. First, they have a good balance between rest and work. Second, they maintain a balance between mental work and physical work. Third, they structure their activities at a good pace that doesn't lead to them feeling overwhelmed and stressed. Fourth, they have the right priorities when it comes to spending time reading the Bible, praying, and being involved in church. Finally, they have learned to trust others and are willing to delegate responsibilities to them.

Are these practices that you have incorporated into your life? If not, you need to ask yourself, "Why do I have this inner drive to continually do more than others do?" The answer is going to involve some deep introspection. Most who have this drive feel a lack of God's love in some area of life. Any time you are willing to put down your emotional baggage and allow God to invade your memories and emotional hurts, He will invade your life with His love.

What a wonderful feeling it is to feel totally accepted and loved by God! I arrived at this point fairly late in my life, but what a day it was! After that experience, I had no trouble knowing that God loved me. I had no trouble trusting Him to be faithful in His love. I had an inner closeness with God unlike any I had experienced before, and this has since grown to an ever deeper intimacy. Parts of me were healed that I didn't even know were weak or ailing.

My desire is for you to come to this same place of total surrender in your life. I encourage you to say to God, "I give everything to You—my life, my relationships, my schedule, my successes and failures, my *everything*. I invite You to take over responsibility for my life and to do whatever is necessary to heal me. Give me today a deep and abiding sense of Your approval, Your love, and Your presence." God will answer that prayer every time.

9. "Unless you are converted and become as little children, you will by no means enter the kingdom of heaven. Therefore whoever humbles himself as this little child is the greatest in the kingdom of heaven" (Matthew 18:3–4). What does it mean to humble yourself as a little child? What areas of your life need that sort of humbling this week?

10. "Humble yourselves in the sight of the Lord, and He will lift you up" (James 4:10). How is being too busy a sign of pride? How will you seek to humble yourself this week?

TODAY AND TOMORROW

Today: Serving God and others can become an area of pride, drawing me away from the Lord.

Tomorrow: This week, I will analyze my schedule and ask God how He wants me to spend my time.

CLOSING PRAYER

Lord, so many of us today are struggling and on the verge of burnout. Our lives seem busier than ever, and we just feel so drained and exhausted all the time. Enable us today to look within ourselves and see those areas where we are trying to "go it alone," do more than You or anyone else expects of us, and are operating outside Your strength and energy. Bring those areas that are out of alignment into sync with Your perfect plan and purpose for us.

NOTES AND
PRAYER REQUESTS

· ·

Use this space to write any key points, questions, or prayer requests from this week's study.

STRENGTH IN TIMES OF PERSECUTION

IN THIS LESSON

Learning: What happens if I am persecuted for my faith in God?

Growing: How should I respond to people who persecute me?

I define *persecution* as a situation that is abusive and painful, but also a situation in which we know that God wants us to stay and for which there seems to be no human resolution. This is especially true if our witness for the Lord is at stake, or if the abuse and pain are being inflicted because our behaviors are based on biblical standards.

I have experienced times of persecution in my life, and I know that they can be intensely painful and emotionally draining. At one point, I experienced opposition and ungodly assaults for nearly three years without any relief. I forged ahead with what I knew God had called me to do by sheer faith, obedience, and endurance. During that time, I became certain about two truths that I believe are related to persecution.

First, God is faithful. God does not abandon us to persecution but walks through persecution with us. He never leaves us nor forsakes us. He is with us at all times, and it is His sustaining love and presence that support us in times of persecution. *Second, persecution is ultimately unimportant.* God's purposes will be accomplished on this earth, and we can either have a part in their accomplishment or fail to have a part. The righteous will prevail. God's plan will come to fruition. We can base our lives on these truths. They can give us the strength to endure whatever persecution comes our way.

Given this, one of the most important things you can do when persecution strikes is to remind yourself that *God is God.* He is in control of you and all circumstances in this world. He will accomplish all that He desires to accomplish. He is all-knowing, all-powerful, ever-present, everlasting, and always willing to extend an infinite and unconditional love. So, when persecution comes, make your first thought, *God is in charge! He will be the victor!*

GOD WILL DEAL WITH HIS ENEMIES

Throughout the Bible, we find many examples of how God deals with His enemies. First, He deals with them *swiftly.* As we read in Psalm 64:7, "But God shall shoot at them with an arrow; suddenly they shall be wounded." Second, God deals with them *decisively.* Moses told the Israelites, "The Egyptians whom you see today, you shall see again no more forever. The Lord will fight for you, and you shall hold your peace" (Exodus 14:13–14). Third, God deals with them *absolutely.* When the sons of Korah rebelled against the commands of the Lord, the earth literally opened and swallowed them up (see Numbers 16).

It is a fearful thing to fight against God, to rebel against God, or to oppose God's people. If you are doing what the Lord has commanded and living in righteousness before the Lord, the enemies who come to persecute you are also making themselves an enemy of God. God defends His people for precisely one reason: *they are His people.*

1. "The LORD . . . troubled the army of the Egyptians. And He took off their chariot wheels, so that they drove them with difficulty; and the Egyptians said, 'Let us flee from the face of Israel, for the LORD fights for them against the Egyptians'" (Exodus 14:24–25). Why did God fight against the Egyptians? How did the Egyptians know it was God whom they were fighting?

"So the LORD saved Israel that day out of the hand of the Egyptians, and Israel saw the Egyptians dead on the seashore. Thus Israel saw the great work which the LORD had done in Egypt; so the people feared the LORD, and believed the LORD and His servant Moses" (Exodus 14:30–31). How can this story encourage you during times of persecution?

KEEP YOUR EYES ON GOD

I believe there are five vital keys to dealing with persecution. *The first is to keep your eyes on the Lord.* Unless you keep your focus on God, you are likely to find yourself feeling angry, bitter, or resentful against those who are persecuting you. Those emotions can be just as damaging as the persecution itself. Don't compound the problem. Stay focused on Jesus!

Some people believe that all forms of persecution come from the enemy. In one regard, they are correct. God never instigates or promotes persecution. But on the other hand, God *does* allow persecution to come into our lives. We see this clearly in the life of Job. God did not authorize the devil's persecution of Job, but He did allow the devil to test him and to bring situations into his life that might well be described as abusive.

One of God's purposes in allowing Job to suffer was to win a battle against the devil. Job's faithfulness and refusal to sin were victories for God over the devil. The Lord also used Satan's persecution in Job's personal life to prepare Job for even greater revelations of Himself.

In nearly every incident of persecution I have witnessed, I have seen God's purposes at work in much the same way. When a person remains faithful to the Lord and refuses to sin, God gains a victory over the devil. The enemy's power is thwarted and his influence is diminished. In addition, a greater strength emerges in the body of Christ, both in the righteous victim and in those who witness the actions of the righteous victim. The victim of persecution who continues to trust in the Lord often has much greater revelations into the Lord's nature, His purposes on this earth, and the relationship that He desires.

2. "The LORD said to Satan, 'Have you considered My servant Job, that there is none like him on the earth, a blameless and upright man, one who fears God and shuns evil?'" (Job 1:8). Why do you think God allowed Satan to persecute His righteous servant?

_____

_____

_____

_____

_____

_____

_____

3. "The LORD said to Satan, 'Behold, all that he has is in your power; only do not lay a hand on his person'" (Job 1:12). Satan can do nothing without first receiving God's permission. What does this reveal about the nature of persecution?

_____

_____

_____

_____

_____

_____

_____

ASK GOD TO STRENGTHEN YOU

A second key principle in dealing with persecution is to ask the Lord to sustain you and strengthen you. The Bible has a great deal to say about those who endure through times of persecution and emerge victorious on the other side. Jesus told His disciples, "If the world hates you, you know that it hated Me before it hated you" (John 15:18). But then He promised to provide them with strength through the coming of the Holy Spirit (see verses 26–27).

Peter also wrote of the strength that God promises to provide in times of persecution. "Beloved, do not think it strange concerning the fiery trial which is to try you, as though some strange thing happened to you; but rejoice to the extent that you partake of Christ's sufferings, that when His glory is revealed, you may also be glad with exceeding joy. If you are reproached for the name of Christ, blessed are you, for the Spirit of glory and of God rests upon you. On their part He is blasphemed, but on your part He is glorified" (1 Peter 4:12–14).

Even as you pray for the Lord to remove the cause of your persecution, pray for the strength to withstand the enemy of your soul until the persecution lifts.

4. "I have fought the good fight, I have finished the race, I have kept the faith" (2 Timothy 4:7). Consider Paul's three metaphors of fighting, marathon running, and having faith. What insights into perseverance does each of these word pictures suggest?

5. "Finally, there is laid up for me the crown of righteousness, which the Lord, the righteous Judge, will give to me on that Day, and not to me only but also to all who have loved His appearing" (2 Timothy 4:8). What does it mean to "love [God's] appearing"? How can that attitude strengthen you during times of persecution?

RECOGNIZE YOU ARE
FIGHTING A SPIRITUAL BATTLE

A third key principle is to know with certainty the battle is the Lord's. You are being persecuted for the cause of Christ and not for an error or an act of your own foolishness. Perhaps the most potent question that you can ask during such times is *who will ultimately get the glory for a victory.* If the person applauded for the victory is anyone other than Christ, it means that mixed motives are in play. To God be the glory for a victory over persecutors—and to no one else!

In fighting a spiritual battle, it is important to remember Paul's words in Ephesians 6:10–18:

> Be strong in the Lord and in the power of His might. Put on the whole armor of God, that you may be able to stand against the wiles of the devil. For we do not wrestle against flesh and blood, but against principalities, against powers, against the rulers of the darkness of this age, against spiritual hosts of wickedness in the heavenly places. Therefore take up the whole armor of God, that you may be able to withstand in the evil day, and having done all, to stand.
>
> Stand therefore, having girded your waist with truth, having put on the breastplate of righteousness, and having shod your feet with the preparation of the gospel of peace; above all, taking the shield of faith with which you will be able to quench all the fiery darts of the wicked one. And take the helmet of salvation, and the sword of the Spirit, which is the word of God; praying always with all prayer and supplication in the Spirit, being watchful to this end with all perseverance and supplication for all the saints.

How you choose to arm yourself in times of persecution is especially important. *Arm yourself with the truth* and make sure you know the truth of the situation from God's perspective. *Arm yourself with righteousness* and make certain you are in right standing with God. *Arm yourself with God's peace* and make your goal true reconciliation and not merely a truce with your persecutors. *Arm yourself with faith* and keep your focus on Jesus.

It is also critical in times of persecution to *arm yourself with the confidence of your salvation and deliverance at God's hand.* Expect the victory to come! Also *arm yourself with the Word of God and endure in prayer.* Be quick to speak the Word of God in the midst of your persecution, and then take it one step further by actually praying for those who are persecuting you. Pray for God to save them. Finally, *persevere in the battle.* Don't give up. Don't give in. Remain solidly grounded in the Lord and stand firm in the strength you receive from Him.

6. Consider each of the pieces of spiritual armor that Paul references in Ephesians 6:14–18. How are you to use the belt of truth, breastplate of righteousness, shoes of the gospel of peace, the shield of faith, and helmet of salvation?

7. What is the only piece of offensive equipment Paul lists in this passage? How does that serve as your weapon along with prayer?

TREAT YOUR PERSECUTORS
WITH LOVE AND KINDNESS

A fourth key principle is to treat your persecutors with godly love and kindness. Your first impulse will likely be to respond to persecution with equal force—to retaliate, to fight, and go on the offensive as you build a strong defense against your persecutors. But the Bible presents a different course of action. Jesus taught that you are to treat your persecutors with kindness—speaking well of them, praying for them, and responding to them with godly love. This is tough to do . . . but it is what you are commanded by the Lord to do!

Jesus also taught that you are to turn the other cheek to those who strike you. You are to "give" in times of persecution, rather than withdraw or wither into silent submission. In many ways, giving is a strong action during persecution. Giving and showing kindness foil the attempts of persecutors. The anger and hatred felt by a persecutor can't help but be thwarted when faced with a loving, giving, praying victim. Ask the Lord to give you the strength to become an active giver in times of persecution, not only an enduring saint.

8. "Love your enemies, do good to those who hate you, bless those who curse you, and pray for those who spitefully use you. To him who strikes you on the one cheek, offer the other also" (Luke 6:27–29). When have you responded to persecution with a counterattack? When have you responded with kindness? What were the results in each case?

9. "And from him who takes away your cloak, do not withhold your tunic either. Give to everyone who asks of you. And from him who takes away your goods do not ask them back" (Luke 6:29–30). Notice that Jesus commands you to not only *endure* persecution but also actively *return* love and kindness in response to that hatred. What does this say about the immense love of God?

LOOK FOR THE VICTORY

A fifth key principle to remember in times of persecution is that there is a reason why you are enduring this season of pain and rejection. Jesus taught, "Blessed are those who are persecuted for righteousness' sake, for theirs is the kingdom of heaven. Blessed are you when they revile and persecute you, and say all kinds of evil against you falsely for My sake. Rejoice and be exceedingly glad, for great is your reward in heaven" (Matthew 5:10–12). The kingdom of heaven is to be gained through your persecution!

Furthermore, Jesus says that a great reward is waiting for you within the kingdom of heaven. There is simply no comparison between the transient anger of persecutors and the glory of eternity. So always keep in mind that persecution is only for a season. As painful as it may be, all persecution is temporary. Eternity awaits!

Look as well for the victory that will come in your life. Your faith will be strengthened, you will gain a greater resolve to win souls, your character will be refined, and you will have greater cause to praise God. Expect the clouds to lift and the glory of God to be revealed when your time of persecution is over!

TODAY AND TOMORROW

Today: I need to remember I am in a spiritual battle against the forces of darkness.

Tomorrow: I will consider all elements of the armor of God and will work on arming myself this week.

CLOSING PRAYER

Heavenly Father, we choose to trust in You in every situation in life—including those times when we are facing persecution. Help us to keep our focus on You during these times. Sustain us and strengthen us as we come to recognize we are engaged in spiritual warfare and the battle ultimately belongs to You. Give us the grace to treat our persecutors with Your godly love and mercy. Help us to remember that our pain will only last a season and that there is a purpose for enduring it. And thank You that we don't have to fight these battles on our own, for You are our strength, our shield, our buckler, our mighty fortress. You are our exceeding great reward.

NOTES AND
PRAYER REQUESTS

Use this space to write any key points, questions, or prayer requests from this week's study.

STRENGTH IN TIMES OF BROKENNESS

IN THIS LESSON

Learning: Why has my life fallen apart?

Growing: What can I possibly gain from being broken?

We all know what it means to be broken—to feel shattered, as if our entire world has fallen apart. We all have times when we don't want to raise our head off the pillow and feel certain the tears will never stop flowing. Brokenness is often accompanied by emptiness—a void that cannot be filled, a sorrow that cannot be comforted, a wound for which there is no balm.

The most painful and difficult times of my life have been when I felt broken. I don't like pain, suffering, or feelings of brokenness any more than anybody else. Certain circumstances in my life have *hurt* . . . at times so intensely I thought I might never heal. But one of the things I have discovered through being broken is that *after* brokenness, we are likely to experience God's greatest presence. After brokenness, our lives can be more fruitful, more purposeful, and more joyful. A genuine blessing can come in the wake of being broken.

AN EXAMPLE OF BROKENNESS IN THE BIBLE

One of the greatest examples of brokenness we have in the Bible is that of the disciple Peter. Perhaps the most famous scene in his life happened the night before Jesus was crucified. Jesus was arrested in the Garden of Gethsemane, and Peter followed at a distance to the place where He was taken. As Peter sat in the courtyard of the high priest's house, a servant girl looked closely at him and said, "This man was with Jesus." But Peter denied knowing Him.

A little while later, someone else saw him and said, "You are one of them." Again, Peter denied the association. A while later, yet another person said, "He was with Him." Peter said, "I don't know what you're talking about." In that moment, Peter came to the full realization he had disowned Jesus in fear when questioned by a few lowly servants. Peter no doubt felt broken in that moment—shattered before God and before the mirror of his own soul.

Peter was talented and gifted in many ways. He was impulsive, strong-willed, outspoken, and physically strong. But he was also self-centered. Yet Jesus still chose Peter. Why? For the same reason He chooses us: *He sees all that we can be.* However, for us to become all that we *can* be, we must experience a "breaking"—a sanding, a sifting, a chiseling of our souls so we truly begin to be conformed to the likeness of Jesus Christ. This is what happened to Peter . . . and it is what happens to each one of us.

116

1. When have you experienced times of brokenness? What did you do? What was the outcome?

2. What blessings have you seen in your own life as a result of times of being broken?

THREE ASPECTS OF
THE BREAKING PROCESS

There are three aspects to God's breaking process. *The first aspect is that God targets the area that needs to be broken.* Each of us has strengths, weaknesses, attitudes, habits, and desires. God knows the specific areas that need to be refashioned and brought to a point of greater maturity. The Lord knew that Peter's impetuous, volatile nature— subject to intense faith one moment and intense fear the next— needed to be refashioned.

We see how the Lord dealt with this in an account from the Gospel of Matthew. Jesus came walking on the water to His disciples, who had been struggling against wind and stormy waters. He called out to them, "Be of good cheer! It is I; do not be afraid" (14:27). Peter answered by saying, "Lord, if it is You, command me to come to You on the water" (verse 28). Jesus invited him, but when Peter stepped out of the boat, he took his eyes off Jesus and onto the wind and waves. He was afraid and began to sink. Jesus stretched out His hand, caught him, and said, "O you of little faith, why did you doubt?" (verse 31). Together, they got into the boat, and the wind ceased. This story reveals how Peter needed to be challenged, even "broken" in this area of his life, so he would not vacillate between faith and fear.

The good news of the Bible is that God created us and knows us. He understands who we are right now but also knows who we can be, what we can do, and what He has fashioned and formed us to do. In times of brokenness, we must trust that God is doing something in us for our eternal good and the fulfillment of His plan in our lives. God does not abandon us in brokenness. He is working during this time to create in us something good.

The second aspect of God's breaking process is that He chooses the tools of our brokenness. Why did Jesus walk on the water? In part, He was setting up a situation in which He could teach Peter and the other disciples. God always brings about the circumstances of our breaking by either engineering a situation that will cause us to confront what He desires to change, or by allowing us to follow the path of sin and error we have chosen. He will give us enough rope so we can entangle ourselves.

God also chooses the tools to break us. He allows us to confront the hurtful remarks or false accusations of people, erroneous negative reports, or people who want to manipulate us for their own purposes. He sometimes even allows our enemies to be tools in His hands. We must realize in times of brokenness that we are not always going to be able to understand God's methods. In fact, most of the time God's ways will confound us. He often chooses the very opposite of what we would choose as a tool with which to work for our good.

The third aspect of God's breaking process is that He controls the pressure. God sets limits on how long the brokenness will last and on the amount of pain and suffering we will endure. God also limits the amount of hurting that He allows us to do. We can hasten the end of a period of brokenness by *yielding to God in submission.* The moment we completely surrender to God, He will begin to reverse the circumstances related to our brokenness and remove the tools that He has used in the breaking process.

We can also be assured that our brokenness will end before it reaches such an intensity that it damages God's purpose for our lives. God will not allow us to be broken to the point where we cannot engage in the ministry He has prepared for us. His purpose is to train us, refashion us, mold us, and conform us to Christ's image—not to destroy us.

So, as you begin to experience a time of brokenness, yield quickly to the Lord. Ask Him what He is seeking to accomplish in your life. Be willing to change what He is asking you to change or embark on what He is calling you to do. Just as Jesus prayed in the Garden of Gethsemane, you need to reach the point where you say, "Father, not my will, but Your will."

3. "Before I formed you in the womb I knew you; before you were born I sanctified you; I ordained you a prophet to the nations" (Jeremiah 1:5). God designed the person you are today. What "rough edges" is He sanding off your character?

4. "For My thoughts are not your thoughts, nor are your ways My ways. . . . For as the heavens are higher than the earth, so are My ways higher than your ways, and My thoughts than your thoughts" (Isaiah 55:8–9). What does it mean that God's ways are higher than our ways? What might this have to do with being broken?

5. What is God's most important "thought" or goal for your life? How have you seen Him gradually working that out in the past?

6. "Cause me to hear Your lovingkindness in the morning, for in You do I trust; cause me to know the way in which I should walk, for I lift up my soul to You" (Psalm 143:8). What must you do if you want to hear God? What is the first step in "knowing" anything?

RESTORATION AFTER BROKENNESS

Once we yield ourselves to the goals the Lord is seeking to accomplish, He will often reveal Himself to us in loving and tender ways. This happened to Peter. After the crucifixion of Christ, the Gospel of John tells us that Peter returned to fishing. Jesus found him by the seashore and said to him, "Peter, do you love Me?" Three times Jesus asked this question, and three times Peter said, "Lord, You know I do!" (see John 21:15–19).

Jesus restored Peter to a relationship with Himself. He forgave him fully for his denial. Three times Peter had denied knowing Jesus, so three times Peter had the opportunity to affirm his love for the Lord. Jesus then gave him something to do: feed and care for "the sheep"—the followers of Jesus who were in need of a leader. Peter finally yielded fully to the Lord's will. As a result, the Lord gave him a supernatural ministry . . . one that was realized in a powerful way beginning on the day of Pentecost (see Acts 2).

The Lord's purpose in brokenness may have many facets to it, but one thing that will always result is a greater opportunity for ministry to others. In the aftermath of our pain, the Lord will give us opportunities to minister to others who are going through similar experiences. Our time of brokenness will prepare us for a time of greater fruitfulness in our ministry.

Brokenness is a pruning process. Jesus taught, "Every branch in Me that does not bear fruit He takes away; and every branch that bears fruit He prunes, that it may bear more fruit" (John 15:2). If you are going to be fruitful in the Lord's kingdom, you will experience a pruning and refining process. The end result will be for your good, for the good of others, and for the expansion of the Lord's kingdom.

7. "I am the true vine, and My Father is the vinedresser. Every branch in Me that does not bear fruit He takes away; and every branch that bears fruit He prunes, that it may bear more fruit" (John 15:1–2). What is involved in pruning a tree or bush? How does this apply to spiritual pruning?

8. In what area would you like to be more fruitful? What might God have to prune away in order to accomplish that fruitfulness in your life?

The Blessings from Brokenness

There are at least five blessings that come from our being broken before the Lord. *The first of these blessings is that we come to understand God better.* We come into a greater understanding of the absolutes of God—that His commandments are exact, His promises are sure, and His methods and timetable are His own. We come to a greater understanding of all of God's attributes.

Second, we come to understand ourselves better. When we are broken, we understand more about our own motivations, desires, and weaknesses. Quite often, we experience an opportunity to ask God's forgiveness in areas of life that we had not thought to confront. We can be freed from confusion about our own past, and God can heal old emotional wounds.

Third, we have increased compassion for others. When we gain new insights about ourselves through brokenness, we emerge with a greater empathy for others and a greater compassion for those who are hurting. Brokenness makes us less critical and judgmental.

Fourth, we have greater enthusiasm for life. When we come to the end of ourselves and stand on the brink of God's unconditional love, we find we have a greater appreciation for all of God's gifts. Life takes on a new zest. We find we are more creative and more willing to express ourselves. We have a greater ability to enjoy our pursuits in life.

Fifth, we have an increased awareness of God's presence. God is with us always, but brokenness makes us more keenly aware of His presence and more sensitive to His desires. In feeling God's presence with us, we have a greater feeling of security.

So, is brokenness worth the pain and struggle? Given blessings such as these, we can all look back at our times of brokenness and say, "I am grateful for all I've been through." The key is turning to the Lord in our brokenness. Those who turn to any other person or thing, or seek to escape, find themselves experiencing only more of the same—and often even greater pain, discouragement, or despair.

Trust God, and God alone, to do His work in you in times when you feel shattered and broken. Allow Him to put you back together in *His* way, in *His* timing, and for *His* purposes.

9. "I will bring the one-third through the fire, will refine them as silver is refined, and test them as gold is tested. They will call on My name, and I will answer them. I will say, 'This is My people'; and each one will say, 'The LORD is my God'" (Zechariah 13:9). Why is silver refined? What is involved in the process of refining it?

10. What areas of your life still need to be refined? How can you help God in the process?

TODAY AND TOMORROW

Today: God uses the breaking process, like the pruning process, to make me more like Jesus.

Tomorrow: I will ask the Lord to show me areas that need His pruning, and will submit to His hand.

CLOSING PRAYER

Lord Jesus, we pray that we will be open to the healing work that You want to do. Target the weaknesses, attitudes, habits, and desires within us that need to be refashioned and brought to a greater level of maturity. Allow us to be willing to listen to those You bring into our lives who speak Your truth, and help us see where we need to change. Help us to be willing to surrender control completely over to You. All You desire is a willing spirit on our part, and You promise to do the rest. So grant us the wisdom, courage, and drive to participate with You in the process.

NOTES AND PRAYER REQUESTS

Use this space to write any key points, questions, or prayer requests from this week's study.

STRENGTH IN TIMES
OF HOPELESSNESS

IN THIS LESSON

Learning: What are some primary causes of hopelessness?

Growing: How should I respond to hopelessness?

Have you ever felt so hopeless or without hope that you wanted to just give up, quit, and walk away? Have you felt so drained that you couldn't concentrate on your next step, let alone how you would handle tomorrow? Have you felt a level of despair that went down into your soul—into your very core as a human being?

If so, you understand some of what David experienced during the low points of his life. You also understand why it is important for us to fortify ourselves with God's inner strength—so we can *survive* those seasons and move on to what's next. When we read the Bible, we see how David's life was a series of ups and downs. He went through high points and low points . . . mountains and valleys.

This is clear even in the psalms that David composed. One moment he is writing of his absolute hope in God, and the next he is writing from the depths of despair. Just consider Psalm 42. David begins by affirming, "My soul thirsts for God, for the living God" (verse 2), but then goes on to question, "I will say to God my Rock, 'Why have You forgotten me? Why do I go mourning because of the oppression of the enemy?'" (verse 9).

There is a false belief that has circulated in the church for centuries—and is still around today—that once we accept Christ and become part of God's family, we cease that up-and-down David experience. We suddenly become steady and serene all the time. Even when we experience difficulties, we are supposed to handle them as if nothing is wrong. The truth is we are still human even as we follow Jesus. We are still affected by our feelings. The best thing we can do during moments of hopelessness is not pretend everything is fine but cry out to God.

It is also helpful to gain an understanding of what causes seasons of hopelessness and despair so we can recognize them more quickly and handle them more effectively. This is what we are going to explore together in this lesson: some of the primary causes of hopelessness in our lives. We are also going to see from Scripture how to seek out God's strength when we find ourselves in those seasons.

1. When have you endured a season of hopelessness or despair? What caused it?

2. On an emotional level, do you tend to have a lot of ups and downs or are you steadier in how you feel? Explain.

WE FEEL HOPELESS WHEN LIFE SEEMS IMPOSSIBLE

If you remember the story of Abraham and Sarah in the Bible, you will recall that God made an incredible promise to both of them. God told Abraham, "I will make you a great nation; I will bless you and make your name great; and you shall be a blessing. I will bless those who bless you, and I will curse him who curses you; and in you all the families of the earth shall be blessed" (Genesis 12:2–3). What a promise to hear from the mouth of God!

The difficulty for Abraham was that he had no children when he received this promise. Also, at this time both he and Sarah were quite old . . . and certainly past their child-bearing years. As you might expect, they became anxious as years went by and the promise remained unfulfilled. In fact, they got so anxious they tried to make the promise happen themselves. Abraham fathered a son through Sarah's maid, Hagar, which only caused more problems.

By the time Abraham was nearing one hundred years of age, despair had set in. God reminded him once more of the promise, but Abraham was in no mood to receive it. "Then Abraham fell on his face and laughed, and said in his heart, 'Shall a child be born to a man who is one hundred years old? And shall Sarah, who is ninety years old, bear a child?'" (17:17). Later, Sarah had a similar response to God's promise: "Therefore Sarah laughed within herself, saying, 'After I have grown old, shall I have pleasure, my lord being old also?'" (18:12).

Imagine being so filled with despair that you laugh at God—that you scoff at His promise to you. But it happens. What I want you to see in this story is that one of the primary causes of hopelessness is a feeling that the circumstances of our lives are impossible. On the one hand, Abraham and Sarah had a promise from God of not only a child but also a nation. On the other hand, they were both way past their childbearing years. They could see no way for God's promise to come true. This caused them to drift downward into despair.

The same thing can happen when the circumstances of your life feel impossible. When you have $10,000 of bills to pay and only $3,000 for paying them, that seems like an impossible situation to resolve. When you desperately want to hold your family together but your spouse has filed for divorce, that seems like an impossible situation. When you are trying to start a career and pave your way in the real world, but the economy has tanked and there are no jobs to be found, that feels like an overwhelmingly impossible situation. And when life feels impossible, it is easy to succumb to feelings of hopelessness and despair.

3. "Jesus looked at them and said to them, 'With men this is impossible, but with God all things are possible'" (Matthew 19:26). What circumstances in your life currently feel impossible? What feelings have those situations led you to experience?

4. When have you seen God accomplish something that seemed impossible?

....

....

....

....

....

....

WE FEEL HOPELESS WHEN IT SEEMS GOD IS ABSENT

Another reason we often drift into hopelessness is when we feel abandoned by God. This can happen for a few different reasons, but it generally happens when we are experiencing the consequences of our sin. Consider the example of Saul. He was the first king of Israel, but he wasted his opportunity. He disobeyed God on multiple occasions. The end result was God stripping the kingdom away from him and anointing David in his place.

God made it clear through the prophet Samuel that Saul was about to lose not only his kingship but also his life: "Because you did not obey the voice of the LORD nor execute His fierce wrath upon Amalek, therefore the LORD has done this thing to you this day. Moreover the LORD will also deliver Israel with you into the hand of the Philistines. And tomorrow you and your sons will be with me" (1 Samuel 28:18–19).

Can you imagine the shock Saul felt in that moment? Here was God's prophet telling him the worst possible news—and it would all be happening within twenty-four hours. As a result, Saul felt abandoned by God and fell to the ground in despair. Now, in reality, God never abandons His people. He has promised us in Scripture that He will continually be present in our lives—"I will never leave you nor forsake you" (Hebrew 13:5). But there are times in our humanness when we will *feel* abandoned, just as Saul did in that moment.

I remember a season in my life when I felt that way. I was reading the Bible and praying every day, but I could not feel a sense of God's presence. Then, all of a sudden, I was pulled down into one of the deepest valleys I can remember. I felt lost. I felt buried in shadows. I would throw myself on my knees at the end of the day and read passages of Scriptures back to God as a way of reminding Him of His promises. It didn't seem to help. I would pull out my hymnbook and try to sing songs of praise. But that didn't work either.

I did everything I could think of to try and get God's attention—to try and receive some kind of relief from the darkness. But I felt no response. It was as if God were nowhere to be found. Intellectually, I knew this wasn't true. I understood God does not forsake His children. But it sure *felt* like it was true. Finally, after a week of total chaos in my life, God turned things around. He revealed Himself to me in a way that was unforgettable and life-changing. It was one of the most incredible encounters with God I have ever experienced.

Feelings of hopelessness do not mean you are hopeless. They are just feelings, and feelings are temporary. If you have a relationship with God through faith in Jesus Christ, His hope and love are *always* available to you.

5. "Behold, I am with you and will keep you wherever you go, and will bring you back to this land; for I will not leave you until I have done what I have spoken to you" (Genesis 28:15). Do you believe that God never abandons His people? Explain.

6. When are times in your life that you felt all alone in this world? What are some powerful ways that God has made His presence known to you?

....

....

....

....

....

....

WE FEEL HOPELESS WHEN DREAMS DIE

Feelings of hopelessness can also invade our lives when it seems our goals and desires will never be fulfilled. Consider the story of Judas. We usually think of him in the context of his betrayal of Christ. But focus for a moment on what he felt toward the end of his life—after his betrayal and Jesus' arrest. "Then Judas . . . seeing that He had been condemned, was remorseful and brought back the thirty pieces of silver to the chief priests and elders. . . . He threw down the pieces of silver in the temple and departed, and went and hanged himself" (Matthew 27:3, 5).

Like many people of his day, Judas believed the Messiah would be a savior in the military sense. He believed the Messiah was destined to free the Jewish people from the control of Rome. It is also likely that Judas believed once Jesus threw off the yoke of Rome and reestablished the glory Israel had earned under King David and King Solomon, he and the other disciples would be given leadership positions in that new and glorious kingdom.

Judas was impatient for Jesus to finally reveal Himself as the promised Messiah and begin the work of fighting back against Rome. This is likely why Judas made his offer to the Pharisees and religious leaders. He was trying to force Jesus to bring about His kingdom by placing Him in a direct confrontation with Rome.

Of course, it all went differently than Judas expected. Jesus was arrested, convicted, and crucified. From Judas's point of view, there was no kingdom. No freedom from Rome. No glory for himself. His dream was shattered. And it sent him into a tailspin of hopelessness and despair.

In the same way, when we have goals or visions, but they come crashing down around us with a finality we can't deny, it can lead us into a time of despair. Or we can be pushed toward hopelessness when our hopes are *delayed*. We have been carrying a dream inside for so long . . . and one day we stop and realize we've been waiting decades and nothing has happened. Our dreams feel so overdue that it seems the goal will never be in sight.

Once again, it is important to remember that a *delay* does not mean the dream will not happen. It could be that God is using the delay to shape your dream into something more in line with His will and plan for your life. You can be assured that if God has given you the dream—just like He gave the dream of a son to Abraham—that He will cause it to occur in His perfect way and timing.

7. "Hope deferred makes the heart sick" (Proverbs 13:12). Which of your biggest hopes or dreams has been deferred?

_____

_____

_____

_____

_____

_____

_____

_____

8. "There are many plans in a man's heart, nevertheless the LORD's counsel—that will stand" (Proverbs 19:21). How do you typically respond when a dream or goal is denied with finality? How can you know if your dream lines up with God's plan for your life?

OVERCOMING DESPAIR AND HOPELESSNESS

It is worth pondering to what end feelings of hopelessness and despair will lead us if not properly addressed. What are the consequences of living without hope? I want to answer this question by first explaining *what is* and then by explaining *what should be.*

First, when we look around today, we see we are living in a largely hopeless society. Look at our cities. No matter how many billions of dollars we throw at the problems being experienced there, they only get worse. There are more and more needs. More and more violence. More and more heartache. We have a culture of hopelessness, which explains why there are so many addictions prevalent today. When people are unable to face the circumstances of their lives, they do whatever they can to escape.

But what *should* things look like? How *should* we deal with hopelessness? The answer is a simple recipe: GOD. He alone is the cure for hopelessness, and He alone remains our source of inner strength when we feel wrapped in hopelessness and despair. I like what Paul writes in Romans: "Now may the God of hope fill you with all joy and peace in believing, that you may abound in hope by the power of the Holy Spirit" (Romans 15:13). God is a God of hope, not of despair. He fills us with hope through the infilling of His Holy Spirit.

This is an incredible truth to remember whenever you are feeling hopeless—when you need strength in the face of despair. The Holy Spirit of God is living within you, and one of His responsibilities is to generate hope within you. No matter your circumstances, or how intense the pain or the warfare around you may seem, the Spirit of God is within you. And if you allow Him, He will generate hope within you by pointing you to your faithful Father.

Not only that, but God will fill you with joy, and peace, and trust in Him, all through the power of the Holy Spirit. No circumstance is hopeless when you have God living inside of you. With God in your life, you never have to give up. You never have to give in to despair. He will grant you the strength you need to continue forward.

9. "The righteous cry out, and the LORD hears, and delivers them out of all their troubles. The LORD is near to those who have a broken heart, and saves such as have a contrite spirit" (Psalm 34:17–18). What promise is given in this passage when you feel hopeless?

10. "Peace I leave with you, My peace I give to you; not as the world gives do I give to you" (John 14:27). How can you access God's peace and hope when you need it?

TODAY AND TOMORROW

Today: I don't have to pretend I don't feel hopelessness or despair in certain seasons.

Tomorrow: I can count on God's promise to produce hope inside me through the power of His Holy Spirit.

CLOSING PRAYER

Heavenly Father, we know that when You are in our lives, there is always a reason to hope. We declare today that our hope is built on nothing less than Jesus' blood and righteousness. We thank You, bless You, and praise You for the ultimate hope that You have given us—salvation through the sacrifice of Your perfect Son on the cross. Help us to keep our focus on You when times feel bleak and overwhelming. Be our comfort and our strength in the midst of the storm. Draw near to us as we draw near to You, so that we can feel Your presence in our lives.

Notes and Prayer Requests

Use this space to write any key points, questions, or prayer requests from this week's study.

THE CALM OF CONTENTMENT

IN THIS LESSON

Learning: What does it mean to be content?

Growing: Why is it important for me to experience contentment as a follower of Christ?

As we come to the conclusion of this study, I think it is worth mentioning again that our modern world is in need of strength. And by that I mean *true* strength, not the false image of strength our society attempts to force on us. Our world is in desperate need of women and men of godly character who can demonstrate the quality of inner strength that can only be achieved through a healthy and meaningful relationship with God.

But what does that strength look like? How does this kind of inner strength express itself in our lives? One way, of course, is that we are not tossed around by the winds and the waves and the storms of life. We can stand firm in the midst of loneliness, or abuse, or criticism, or hopelessness and not falter. But another expression of inner strength can be summed up in a word we often use but don't always adequately comprehend: *contentment*.

The apostle Paul wrote about contentment in 1 Timothy 6, and in this final lesson, we are going to look more closely at the first half of that chapter. But the heart of Paul's thoughts on contentment can be found in these verses: "Now godliness with contentment is great gain. For we brought nothing into this world, and it is certain we can carry nothing out. And having food and clothing, with these we shall be content" (verses 6–8).

You have probably heard the phrase "godliness with contentment is great gain," but what does that mean? What does it look like in our lives? To answer these questions, we will explore together the *scope of contentment*, the *search for contentment*, the *source of contentment*, and the steps we need to take to *secure contentment* in our lives.

1. What's the first thing that comes to mind when you hear the word *contentment*?

2. Who are some people you would describe as content? What qualities or attributes do they possess that make them appear to be content?

....

....

....

....

....

....

THE SCOPE OF CONTENTMENT

To begin, we need to make sure we understand what is meant when we talk about *contentment*. Many people today have the wrong idea about what contentment is and why it is important. In particular, many people confuse contentment with the practice of following the status quo. They understand contentment as being passive . . . as going with the flow. In this line of thinking, to be content is to believe life is "good enough" and there is no need to strive for anything better. It is better to simply sit back and relax.

Let me be clear that this is not the biblical meaning of contentment. If contentment only had to do with being satisfied in our present circumstances, it would mean we have no reason or motivation to improve ourselves—including our spiritual condition! It would mean there is no reason for us to pursue spiritual maturity. We would simply be content with our current state, even if it includes addictions or sin or other elements that are destructive.

No, once again, that is not contentment. That is simply being passive and lazy. In contrast, I believe the best definition for contentment is *realizing that God has provided all we need for our present happiness.* In other words, God has already provided whatever we need today to make us into the people whom He desires us to be. Notice the past

141

tense—it's already settled. Already accomplished. God has already made provision for everything we need.

Here is another way to think about it. Contentment doesn't mean that we are called to be satisfied with our circumstances no matter what they are. Content means we are to realize that God desires good things for our lives and is personally involved in them. If our present circumstances are not right—if they are not good for us or those around us—we can trust He intends to make them better and has a plan to accomplish that goal.

In the end, this means we should take action to improve ourselves and make a positive influence on our circumstances. But we don't have to be anxious, fearful, or frustrated as we do this. We can be content that God is personally involved and will provide what we need.

3. How do you respond to the definition of contentment included above? Does that definition apply to you currently? Explain.

4. "His divine power has given to us all things that pertain to life and godliness, through the knowledge of Him who called us by glory and virtue" (2 Peter 1:3). How can you know that God has already provided *everything you need* to serve Him?

THE SEARCH FOR CONTENTMENT

We all understand that people today want to be happy. However, we all define happiness in different ways. Some people are looking for pleasure. Others are looking for peace. Still others will only consider themselves to be happy if they find meaning, purpose, and fulfillment. What people are really looking for is *contentment*. Whether people understand it or not, there is a universal longing in our hearts to know God is present in our circumstances. We need to know we are not alone and are not responsible to make everything in our lives turn out well.

This is what people want. It doesn't matter what nationality they are, or how old they are, or whether they are educated, wealthy, self-confident, or anything else. People are searching for contentment. The problem is that most of us look for it in the wrong places.

For example, think of a single woman in her thirties. She is convinced that she will be happy if only she can find that handsome, rich, spiritual young man of her dreams. So she prays for God to send him her way, believing marriage will bring contentment.

Or consider a man who grew up in a small town in the Midwest. He feels that if he could just get out of that claustrophobic community and travel the world, he would be content with his life. If he could just see what is really out there . . . he would finally be happy.

There are those who believe they can find contentment if they have a child. There are teenagers who think they will find contentment once they are able to break free from the shackles of their parents and leave home. Others believe contentment means finally getting that promotion at work or not being under the thumb of their boss any longer.

And, of course, most people believe they would finally be content if they just had a little more money. They think, "If I could just be a little bit wealthy, everything would be all right. I don't have to be a billionaire, but just have enough to meet my needs—and maybe throw in a few luxuries I've always wanted. Then I would finally be happy. I would finally be content."

The apostle Paul throws a bucket of cold water on all these "if only" statements. In his letter to Timothy, he writes, "Those who desire to be rich fall into temptation and a snare, and into many foolish and harmful lusts which drown men in destruction and perdition" (1 Timothy 6:9). The majority of our searching for contentment is unfruitful. Often, it is directly harmful. This is because we are searching in the wrong places. Even those of us within the church.

This is a shame, because the world needs to see God's people living in contentment. The world needs to see Christians who express the inner strength of contentment. Why? Because the world needs to see that contentment is possible! Our culture is filled with anxious, frustrated, unhappy people who are desperately searching for answers. They need to see the only true answer—the only true source for contentment—is found in Christ.

5. "No one can serve two masters; for either he will hate the one and love the other, or else he will be loyal to the one and despise the other. You cannot serve God and [money]" (Matthew 6:24). Why is it easy to believe that wealth brings contentment?

6. Who does Jesus say that you are *really* serving when you chase after riches? Why do you think He says you can't serve God and money at the same time?

THE SOURCE OF TRUE CONTENTMENT

My guess is that you already know the source of true contentment. The only real source of contentment in this world is *Christ*. Still, we can go deeper when it comes to accessing that source. Sadly, today there are plenty of men and women who know Christ—who have been given eternal life through the death and resurrection of Jesus—and yet do not have contentment.

So, how do we actually *experience* contentment? How do we take hold of it? *First, we must have a relationship with God as our heavenly Father.* Notice here that I say we need to have a relationship with God as our *Father*—not with God as a supreme being or as the Creator of the universe. We need to know God as a father. We need this emotional connection.

Many people fail to realize that God is an emotional being. He is a *person* in that sense. And because He is a person, we can build a relationship with Him. We can know Him and be known by Him. As I once heard someone say, "To long for another person is to experience the same emotion God has for you in that moment."

Second, to experience contentment in a real way, we must recognize God as our all-sufficient provider. As long as we question whether God cares about us, we will never have contentment. As long we wonder whether God is really able to provide for our needs, we will never find the happiness we desire. As long as we doubt whether God is willing to hear and answer our prayers, we won't have the peace and security the Lord wants us to have.

Contentment is the knowledge that not only does God personally care about us but that He is also all-sufficient, inexhaustible, and ever-available to us. In every moment of life, He is able to provide what we need. Furthermore, experiencing contentment requires us to *seek out* God as our provider. This means we turn to Him when we are in need. We don't just wait passively or try to figure out things on our own. We reach out to God as our ultimate provider.

Finally, to experience contentment, we must regularly and consistently rely on God's faithfulness. Another way to say it is that we must simply trust in Him. Now, the idea of trusting God and actually putting that into practice are two different things. We all know that we are supposed to trust God. We all say that we want to trust Him. But acting on that trust is different and much harder. The core element in building that trust with God is reminding ourselves of all the ways He has been faithful in the past—of all the ways He has earned our trust.

7. "Therefore, pray: 'Our Father in heaven, hallowed be Your name. Your kingdom come. Your will be done on earth as it is in heaven'" (Matthew 6:9–10). What is significant about the fact that Jesus *instructs* us to address God as our father?

8. "For you did not receive the spirit of bondage again to fear, but you received the Spirit of adoption by whom we cry out, 'Abba, Father'" (Romans 8:15). How would you describe what it means to live out a personal relationship with God as "father"?

Securing Contentment

Let's conclude this study by exploring some practical steps we can take to secure the contentment that God wants us to have and make it a reality each and every day.

First, repentance to God is necessary in securing contentment. If you are not regularly in the practice of repenting of your sins before God, sooner or later guilt will begin to creep into your life. You will start believing yourself unworthy of God's provision. You will start to wonder if God really does want to know you after all. This will lead to feelings of discontent. Therefore, search your heart on a regular basis and get rid of anything that doesn't belong there. Repent of your sin before God . . . your loving heavenly Father.

Second, rebuild your thought structures. By this, I simply mean you should start thinking about your life with God at the center—not you at the center. There is no such thing as experiencing contentment when life revolves around you. So make sure your life revolves around God and what He wants.

Third, refocus your emotions. All too often, you may find that your desires and your emotional attachments are based on yourself. Instead, you need to train yourself to desire God. To long for God and desire His presence. Prayer is a good example of what I mean. All too often I hear people pray, "God, thank You for a good night's rest. Please bless my family today. Please bless me at my job today. Please meet my financial needs today. Please give me these specific things I desire and I have been waiting patiently to receive." On and on it goes.

I'm going to say this bluntly: this kind of prayer ignores God. Instead of leading to contentment, it just builds up a desire in your heart for more and more blessings. More and more stuff. If that describes your prayer life or your relationship with God, you need to refocus your emotions so that you desire *Him*, not what He can give you.

Finally, to secure contentment in your life, you need to redirect your goals. Each of us has many goals in life. Each of us has several things we are hoping to achieve or accomplish not just in the long-term but in the short-term as well. And that's okay. It is positive, because our goals are one of the means that God uses to direct our steps. But you need to ask yourself this question: *Is my main goal to know God's will for my life?*

This should always be your number-one goal: to know God's will *and to do it.* Your desire should be to understand God's will for your life today, right this moment, and then take steps to accomplish His goals. You need to do this before you focus on your own agenda. In the end, pursuing His will and plans leads to contentment—and to greater inner strength.

9. "Direct my steps by Your word, and let no iniquity have dominion over me" (Psalm 119:133). Which of the steps listed above do you need to take? Why?

10. What obstacles are currently hindering your ability to feel greater contentment?

TODAY AND TOMORROW

Today: I can take specific steps to move toward true contentment in my life.

Tomorrow: I can be a shining example to an anxious world that contentment is possible.

CLOSING PRAYER

Lord God, so many of us are like a stagnant pool—slick, slimy, and devoid of life. We wonder why we are not happy. We cry out for You to do something to fill the void. We fail to recognize You use such times of discontentment to move us forward, get us to engage with others, and look to the needs of others instead of our own. We know that as long as we center life on ourselves, we will never experience contentment. So open our eyes today to any area where we have taken our focus off You. Make us into living, flowing, abundant streams that reproduce Your life. Be our source of contentment today as we choose to follow You.

Notes and Prayer Requests

Use this space to write any key points, questions, or prayer requests from this week's study.

LEADER'S GUIDE

Thank you for choosing to lead your group through this Bible study from Dr. Charles F. Stanley on *Developing Inner Strength*. The rewards of being a leader are different from those of participating, and it is our prayer that your own walk with Jesus will be deepened by this experience. During the twelve lessons in this study, you will be helping your group members explore and discuss key themes about how they can gain God's strength in times of loneliness, fear, criticism, guilt, frustration, burnout, brokenness, and even persecution. There are multiple components in this section that can help you structure your lessons and discussion time, so please be sure to read and consider each one.

BEFORE YOU BEGIN

Before your first meeting, make sure your group members each have a copy of *Developing Inner Strength* so they can follow along in the study guide and have their answers written out ahead of time. Alternately, you can hand out the study guides at your first meeting and give the group members some time to look over the material and ask any preliminary questions. During your first meeting, be sure to send a sheet around the room and have the members write down their name, phone number, and email address so you can keep in touch with them during the week.

To ensure everyone has a chance to participate in the discussion, the ideal size for a group is around eight to ten people. If there are more than ten people, break up the bigger group into smaller subgroups. Make sure the members are committed to participating each week, as this will help create stability and help you better prepare the structure of the meeting.

At the beginning of each meeting, you may wish to start the group time by asking the group members to provide their initial reactions to the material they have read during the week. The goal is to just get the group members' preliminary thoughts—so encourage them at this point to keep their answers brief. Ideally, you want everyone in the group to get a chance to share some of their thoughts, so try to keep the responses to a minute or less.

Give the group members a chance to answer, but tell them to feel free to pass if they wish. With the rest of the study, it's generally not a good idea to have everyone answer every question—a free-flowing discussion is more desirable. But with the opening icebreaker questions, you can go around the circle. Encourage shy people to share, but don't force them. Also, try to keep any one person from dominating the discussion so everyone will have the opportunity to participate.

WEEKLY PREPARATION

As the group leader, there are a few things you can do to prepare for each meeting:

- *Be thoroughly familiar with the material in the lesson.* Make sure you understand the content of each lesson so you know how to structure the group time and are prepared to lead the group discussion.

- *Decide, ahead of time, which questions you want to discuss.* Depending on how much time you have each week, you may not be able to reflect on every question. Select specific questions that you feel will evoke the best discussion.

- *Take prayer requests.* At the end of your discussion, take prayer requests from your group members and then pray for one another.

- *Pray for your group.* Pray for your group members throughout the week and ask God to lead them as they study His Word.

- *Bring extra supplies to your meeting.* The members should bring their own pens for writing notes, but it's a good idea to have extras available for those who forget. You may also want to bring paper and additional Bibles.

STRUCTURING THE GROUP DISCUSSION TIME

You will need to determine with your group how long you want to meet each week so you can plan your time accordingly. Generally, most groups like to meet for either sixty minutes or ninety minutes, so you could use one of the following schedules:

SECTION	60 Minutes	90 Minutes
WELCOME (group members arrive and get settled)	5 minutes	10 minutes
ICEBREAKER (group members share their initial thoughts regarding the content in the lesson)	10 minutes	15 minutes
DISCUSSION (discuss the Bible study questions you selected ahead of time)	35 minutes	50 minutes
PRAYER/CLOSING (pray together as a group and dismiss)	10 minutes	15 minutes

As the group leader, it is up to you to keep track of the time and keep things moving according to your schedule. If your group is having a good discussion, don't feel the need to stop and move on to the next question. Remember, the purpose is to pull together ideas and share unique insights on the lesson. Encourage everyone to participate, but don't be concerned if certain group members are more quiet. They may just be internally reflecting on the questions and need time to process their ideas before they can share them.

GROUP DYNAMICS

Leading a group study can be a rewarding experience for you and your group members—but that doesn't mean there won't be challenges. Certain members may feel uncomfortable in discussing topics that they consider very personal and might be afraid of being called on. Some members might have disagreements on specific issues. To help prevent these scenarios, consider establishing the following ground rules:

- If someone has a question that may seem off topic, suggest that it is discussed at another time, or ask the group if they are okay with addressing that topic.

- If someone asks a question to which you do not know the answer, confess that you don't know and move on. If you feel comfortable, you can invite the other group members to give their opinions or share their comments based on personal experience.

- If you feel like a couple of people are talking much more than others, direct questions to people who may not have shared yet. You could even ask the more dominating members to help draw out the quiet ones.

- When there is a disagreement, encourage the members to process the matter in love. Invite members from opposing sides to evaluate their opinions and consider the ideas of the other members. Lead the group through Scripture that addresses the topic, and look for common ground.

When issues arise, encourage your group to follow these words from Scripture: "Love one another" (John 13:34), "If it is possible, as much as depends on you, live peaceably with all men" (Romans 12:18), "Whatever things are true ... noble ... pure ... lovely ... if there is any virtue and if there is anything praiseworthy—meditate on these things" (Philippians 4:8), and "Be swift to hear, slow to speak, slow to wrath" (James 1:19). This will make your group time more rewarding and beneficial for everyone who attends.

Thank you again for your willingness to lead your group. May God reward your efforts and dedication, equip you to guide your group in the weeks ahead, and make your time together in *Developing Inner Strength* fruitful for His kingdom.

Also Available from Charles F. Stanley

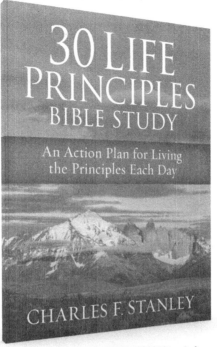

9780310082521   Softcover

30 LIFE PRINCIPLES BIBLE STUDY
An Action Plan for Living the Principles Each Day

During his many years of ministry, Dr. Charles Stanley has faithfully highlighted the 30 life principles that have guided him and helped him to grow in his knowledge, service, and love of God. In this Bible study, you will explore each of these principles in depth and learn how to make them a part of your everyday life. As you do, you will find yourself growing in your relationship with Christ and on the road to the future God has planned for you.

Available now at your favorite bookstore.

Also Available in the
CHARLES F. STANLEY
Bible Study Series

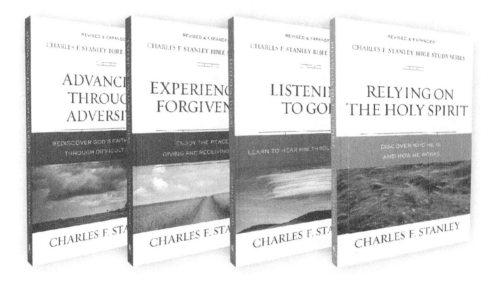

Each study draws on Dr. Stanley's many years of
teaching the guiding principles found in God's Word,
showing how we can apply them in practical ways to
every situation we face. This edition of the series has
been completely revised and updated, and includes
two brand-new lessons from Dr. Stanley.

Available now at your favorite bookstore.
More volumes coming soon.